AUGUSTAN ROME

Current and forthcoming titles in the Classical World Series

Classical World Series

AUGUSTAN ROME

Andrew Wallace-Hadrill

Bristol Classical Press

General Editor: John H. Betts
Series Editor: Michael Gunningham

This impression 2002

First published in 1993 by
Bristol Classical Press
an imprint of
Gerald Duckworth & Co. Ltd
61 Frith Street
London W1D 3JL
e-mail: inquiries@duckworth-publishers.co.uk
Website: www.ducknet.co.uk

Reprinted 1994, 1995, 1997, 1998, 2000, 2001

A catalogue record for this book is available
from the British Library

ISBN 1-85399-138-4

Printed in Great Britain by
Antony Rowe Ltd

Contents

List of Illustrations

Preface

Augustan Rome is a vast subject, on which much has been said, and much remains to be said. In a slim volume like this one cannot hope even to introduce every aspect of the subject. An outline narrative of the period by itself would use up the space available, let alone any attempt to introduce the poetry and art of the period. Good outlines are already available. What I have attempted is not an introduction, but an interpretative essay. I hope that it will make sense to someone relatively new to the subject, at sixth-form or first-year University level. My aim is to give the reader some sense of the way in which the victory of Octavian at Actium transformed Rome and Roman life. My chronological scope is 31 BC–AD 14; the geographical focus is on the city of Rome, and I have deliberately left the provinces and their administration, the armies and their conquests and defeats, on one side. I have tried to set political changes in the context of their impact on Roman values, on the imaginative world of poetry, on the visual world of art and on the fabric of the city of Rome. Anyone who knows Paul Zanker's *The Power of Images in the Age of Augustus* will see my debt to him. I have also tried to show how this transformation was a slow and gradual process: the Augustan age is one of experiment. The viewpoint developed here is a personal one. Innocent readers should beware: my text picks its way through minefields of scholarly controversy. It should be read, like all historical writing, cautiously and critically. Augustus is far too complex for any one interpreter's view to rate as authoritative or final. I only hope that my picture will stimulate the reader to construct his or her own Augustus.

Friends have helped greatly by their comments on an early draft: Michael Gunningham (as Series Editor), Jane Gardner, Fergus Millar and Tessa Rajak (each of whom disagreed with me most at the points at which they were most knowledgeable), and my wife Jo, whose distaste for history I have here struggled to overcome.

A. W-H., December 1992

Chronological Overview

The narrative of the rise of Octavian/Augustus is exciting, but complex. The classic modern treatment is Ronald Syme, *The Roman Revolution* (1939). Shakespeare's *Julius Caesar* and *Antony and Cleopatra* show extraordinary historical grasp as well as drama. Those with no knowledge of the period may start by reading this summary.

BC

63   Gaius Octavius, the future Augustus, born in Rome. Father Octavius praetor in 61, died in 58. Mother Atia, daughter of Julius Caesar's sister, Julia.

44   Julius Caesar assassinated. Octavius inherits most of great-uncle's fortune and name, becoming Gaius Julius Caesar Octavianus (Octavian). Raises Caesar's veterans against the consul Marcus Antonius (Antony), supported by Cicero in public attacks on Antony (*Philippics*).

43   Octavian defeats Antony at Munda, then realigns and forms triumvirate with Antony and Lepidus (November). Cicero heads list of victims of judicial murders (proscriptions).

42   Brutus, Cassius and anti-Caesarians defeated at Philippi. Division of empire: Antony takes East, Octavian West, Lepidus Africa.

41   Octavian distributes lands of 18 Italian cities to veterans. Antony in East, meets Cleopatra at Tarsus. Antony's brother Lucius champions dispossessed landowners and others in Italy against Octavian.

40   Lucius Antonius defeated after siege at Perusia. Octavian and Antony reconciled at Brundisium: Antony marries Octavian's sister Octavia to seal pact. Sextus Pompeius, son of Pompey the Great, threatens food-supply to Rome from base in Sicily. Octavian marries Scribonia, sister of Sextus' father-in-law.

39   Sextus Pompeius placated at treaty of Misenum. Daughter Julia born to Octavian and Scribonia.

37   Octavian divorces Scribonia, marries Livia, already mother of Tiberius and pregnant with Drusus.

36   Octavian (with friend Agrippa) defeats Sextus Pompeius at battle of Naulochus off Sicily. Lepidus disgraced for ambiguous role in campaign. Antony's invasion of Parthia, supported by Cleopatra, ends in retreat; conquest of Armenia claimed.

34   Antony and Cleopatra reorganise kingdoms of east, proclaiming their twin sons kings ('donations of Alexandria').

32   Octavian seizes Antony's will from Vestal Virgins and reads in public. Engineers oath of allegiance in campaign against Antony by all cities of Italy (*tota Italia*). Antony divorces Octavia.

31   Antony prepares invasion armada in gulf of Ambracia. Octavian blockades, defeats Antony's fleet and armies at Actium. Antony and Cleopatra escape to Egypt.

30   Octavian enters Alexandria; Antony and Cleopatra commit suicide. Egypt becomes Roman province.

29   Octavian returns to Rome, celebrates triple triumph.

28   Octavian starts 'handover' of power. Restores 82 temples in Rome. Builds Mausoleum.

27   January 13, Octavian 'restores' power to senate and people. Takes name Augustus, and control of vital military provinces.

26-4 Augustus campaigns in Spain.

25   Octavia's son Marcellus marries Julia.

23   Near death of Augustus. Resigns consulship, in future holds 'tribunician power'. Death of Marcellus.

22   Conspiracy of Caepio and Murena foiled (dated by some to 23 as part of supposed constitutional crisis).

21   Julia marries Agrippa. Augustus campaigns in East.

20   Diplomatic victory over Parthia; captured legionary standards returned to Tiberius.

19   Augustus returns to Rome, celebrates not with triumph but altar and triumphal arch.

18   Legislative programme passed (*leges Juliae*) including laws on marriage and sexual conduct.

17   Secular Games celebrate purification of Rome and new age. Augustus adopts (implicitly as heirs) Gaius and Lucius, sons of Julia and Agrippa.

16   Augustus starts Gallic/German campaign. Tiberius and Drusus command against Alpine tribes.

13   Augustus returns from northern front. Celebrates not with triumph but dedication of Altar of Augustan Peace.

12   Agrippa dies. Augustus becomes Pontifex Maximus on death of long-disgraced Lepidus.

11	Julia marries Tiberius, still busy with northern campaigns.
9	Drusus dies on campaign in Germany. Tiberius continues campaign.
7	Tiberius returns to Rome, celebrating triumph.
6	Tiberius made Augustus' colleague in tribunician power. Demonstrations in theatre in favour of Gaius and Lucius. Tiberius retires to Rhodes against Augustus' will.
2	Scandal of Julia's adultery, Julia exiled. Augustus acclaimed as Pater Patriae – Father of his Country. Temple of Mars the Avenger dedicated in new Forum.
1	Gaius takes command in new eastern campaign.

AD

1	Gaius becomes consul aged 19 (22 years early).
2	Lucius dies on way to command in Spain. Tiberius returns to Rome.
4	Gaius wounded at siege of Artogira in Armenia, dies in Lycia. Tiberius reappointed to tribunician power.
6	Revolt of Pannonia; Tiberius takes command.
8	Disgrace of younger Julia, granddaughter of Augustus. Ovid exiled to Tomi.
9	Loss of three legions under Varus in German ambush.
14	Augustus dies, and declared god, Divus Augustus. Tiberius, after much-advertised hesitations, takes over.

The House of the Caesars

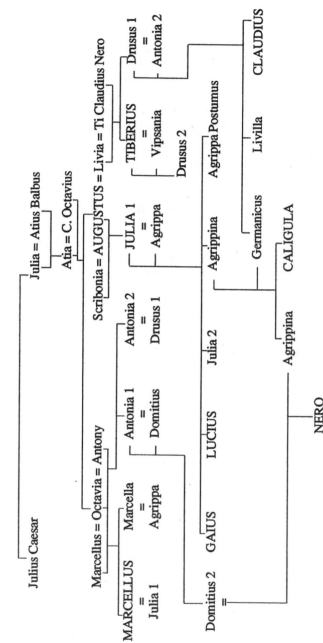

Chapter 1
The Myth of Actium

Augustus gave the Roman world a new order. This meant not just new rules in the game of politics, but a new sense of what Rome was and what being Roman meant. His new order emerged from a transformation of an old order, which we can call the Republic: wrapped up in that expression is a whole set of traditions and values, as well as a system of government. Augustus' new order was rooted in a new mythology: in emotionally charged symbols which touched on deep fears and hopes, on values so basic that all Romans shaped their lives around them. At the heart of that mythology was the battle by which Augustus established his dominance over the Roman world, the battle of Actium. We may be tempted to think of it as the symbol of the triumph of military despotism; but that was not quite how Romans were supposed to think of it. It was a symbol of salvation, of the rescue of Rome from destruction.

The assassination of Caesar in 44 BC had left Rome in chaos. Two main contestants rapidly emerged for the control of the Caesarian cause: Caesar's second in command, one of the consuls of that year, Marcus Antonius (Antony), and Caesar's great-nephew and heir, Gaius Octavius, who promptly renamed himself Caesar, adding for good measure, when his 'father' was declared a god, the title Divi filius, son of the god (Fig. 1). Modern historians, to avoid confusion, prefer to call him Octavian, remembering, clumsy though it seems, to call him Augustus after his final name-change of 27 BC. For 14 years Octavian and Antony oscillated between enmity and alliance; joining forces to seize control of the empire in a coup officialised as the triumvirate (a threesome with Lepidus), yet from the first competing with each other fiercely, and only patching up their allied front by repeated pacts and compromises, including the marriage of Octavian's sister Octavia to Antony. Actium could come as no surprise, as the final showdown between two dynasts who for so long had fenced for mastery of the Roman world.

What was a long-standing battle for personal dominance even so took on the colours of a battle for the traditional values and freedoms of the Roman citizen. Liberty was by no means a dead cause. Caesar had been killed by men who believed *libertas* could be rescued from tyranny.

1

Fig. 1 Coin issued by Octavian c. 40 BC. Octavian describes himself as CAESAR DIVI F (son of god), and portrays Julius Caesar on the other face as DIVOS IULIUS (God Julius).

Their cause did not disappear with Brutus and Cassius at Philippi in 42 BC. Antony's own brother Lucius, as consul in 41, proclaimed the cause of liberty against Octavian, in a cynical attempt to exploit the anger arising from Octavian's massive confiscations of land in Italy for redistribution to his veterans. Lucius was crushed at the siege of Perusia in Umbria (40), leaving a legacy of resentment against Octavian (men said he had offered 300 prisoners in sacrifice to the shades of Caesar). A new rallying point for 'republicans' emerged: Sextus Pompey, son of the Pompey at the foot of whose statue Caesar died. The young Pompey matched against the young Caesar: each could proclaim his *pietas*, his devotion to his father's memory. Sextus assembled off Sicily an impressive navy, thanks in part to inherited connections with the pirate chiefs whom his father had defeated. His blockade of the crucial corn route to Rome caused Octavian extreme difficulties for five years. Octavian's marriage to Scribonia (Sextus was married to Scribonia's niece) was one attempt to neutralise this threat. The elimination of Sextus took a long campaign, the traces of which are still visible around the Bay of Naples in the engineering works which converted Lake Avernus into a haven for training crews. When Octavian, together with his captain Agrippa, defeated Sextus off Sicily at the battle of Naulochus in 36 BC, he proclaimed (reviving memories of Spartacus) a victory over runaway slaves; but that was, of course, to disguise what might have been called a victory over liberty, the cause which he himself was anxious to espouse against Antony. After Actium, Octavian's coins declared him the champion of the liberty of the Roman people, LIBERTATIS PR VINDEX;

before the battle both sides were equally anxious to claim this honour.

As the historians describe it, Actium was not much of a battle. Antony had gathered a formidable armada of 500 ships on the west coast of Greece in preparation for an invasion of Italy that would 'liberate' Rome, as he saw it, from the grip of Octavian (Fig. 2). An important component of the armada was the squadron of galleys provided by Cleopatra: the Ptolemies of Egypt were renowned for the advanced technology of their ship building, of which the secret (still hidden to us) lay in multiplying up the oar-power from the standard three-banked trireme. Octavian too had an impressive fleet, battle-hardened and strengthened after the defeat of the navy of Sextus Pompeius, and an outstanding commander in Agrippa. But his triremes were techni-cally outclassed by the four-to ten-bankers of Antony, vast hulks which men compared to Cycladic islands (Virgil, *Aeneid* 8.691). Octavian anticipated the invasion by blockading Antony's fleet while it was still assembling. His strategy was to keep the war out of Italy, and to deprive Antony's galleys of the advantage of momentum by trapping them in the narrow mouth of the gulf of Ambracia.

The gulf might seem the perfect spot to assemble an armada against Italy. A place of haunting beauty, its salt-flats and tranquil blue waters, ringed by rugged mountains, still offer refuge to wild life and rare breeds of pelican. The gulf cuts 20 miles inland; at its mouth it is

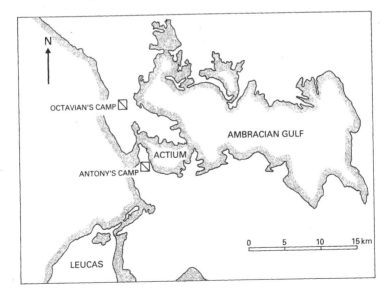

Fig. 2 Location of the battle of Actium.

guarded by two promontories which squeeze together like crab's claws, leaving a narrow and easily defensible passageway only a few hundred metres wide. The lower promontory of Actium, now the local airport, was where Antony's army encamped, near a temple to Apollo. Octavian, advancing down the coast from Corfu and the north, seized the upper promontory for his own camp. The site is marked by the memorial he built and decorated with the spoils of victory, the massive bronze beaks of Antony's galleons (Fig. 3). Below it he built a City of Victory, Nicopolis, where a celebratory festival was long held.

Stormy winds delayed the engagement for four days, but on the fifth (2 September, 31 BC) calm weather offered ideal conditions. The battle should have been magnificent. 'The hands of the world came together', according to Propertius (*Elegies* 4.6.19); in sheer scale it was indeed the largest assemblage of naval forces in antiquity. But the battle was lost before they engaged. Antony hung back, indecisive (one of the wilder stories was that his flagship had been immobilised by a sucking fish with the remarkable property of stopping ships in their tracks).

Fig. 3 View of the victory monument put up by Octavian above Nicopolis near Actium. Dedicated to Neptune and Mars in commemoration of a victory on land and sea, it displayed the largest of the bronze rams from Antony's ships. Slots in the stonework reveal the massive size of these rams, coming from ships with 4 to 10 banks of oars.

Cleopatra waited for a breeze to blow up, hoisted sail and fled with her squadron, the pallor of death, in the poet's vision, foreshadowed on her face (Virgil, *Aeneid* 8.709). Antony sat in her ship three days without speaking, his head between his hands. He had deserted his armada before it had been defeated, and left his 19 legions standing by inactive. His spirit was broken.

The demoralisation of Antony and his forces had been progressive. His commanders had been slipping away gradually for months – till he could no longer trust them. One, Domitius Ahenobarbus, left in a dinghy immediately before the battle: Antony sent his baggage after him. Others like Munatius Plancus had come with horror stories of life at Cleopatra's court. Plancus complained that he had been forced to dance naked at a drunken party, painted blue in the guise of the sea-god Glaucus. Some of the stories of the high life became legendary. The pearl Cleopatra is supposed to have dissolved in vinegar and drunk was in fulfilment of a bet with Antony, who was confessed beaten, a bad omen on the eve of Actium.

The survival of such stories reflects a double victory won at Actium. As well as the naval battle, there was a propaganda battle, a battle for 'hearts and minds'. The propaganda war was fought both before and after the battle. Antony was and is its victim. Octavian, according to the historian Dio, told his troops before the battle that what mattered in war was not the size of your armament, but the justice of the cause you fought for. His triumph was to persuade not only his own side, but much of Antony's, of the superior justice of his cause. That was achieved by systematic denigration of Antony. Here Octavian could build on what he had learnt from that master of persuasion, Cicero, whose savage attacks in the sequel to Caesar's death, the *Philippics*, aimed consistently at undermining Antony's legitimacy, not least by travestying his personal life. Cicero's Antony, lurching into the Forum after a night's drinking to spew over the rostra, and driving down the roads of Italy with a cortege of actresses and prostitutes, is the origin of Octavian's Antony, a Hercules unmanned by Omphale, swapping his lionskin for silk dresses, besotted with Cleopatra, a Roman general no more.

It is no longer possible to recover the real Antony behind the denigration (though both Plutarch and Shakespeare recognised his stature). Perhaps Antony, aware of the colourful lifestyle of the Roman upper classes, underestimated the significance of such accusations, and the vein of Roman puritanism Octavian was able to play on. Or perhaps he thought it safe, in the exotic world of the Greek East, to play up the role of the new Dionysus, god of liberation, and to stage great pageants in the fashion of the Eastern courts.

> The barge she sat in, like a burnish'd throne,
> Burn'd on the water: the poop was beaten gold;
> Purple the sails, and so perfumed that
> The winds were love-sick with them...
> (Shakespeare, *Antony and Cleopatra* II ii, 199ff.)

The effect was intoxicating, on Antony as on the crowds. But love-sick or not, he needed Cleopatra's support. After the failure of the Parthian expedition that was to have made him the Roman Alexander (36 BC), he needed the wealth of the Ptolemies, as well as their navy, and in 34 BC supported Cleopatra's ambitions in declaring her Queen of Kings, and his children by her Kings (Fig. 4).

The romance and the Hollywood lifestyle of the stars are essential ingredients of the myth of Actium. They played a vital part in discrediting Antony at the time, and so of losing him the battle. But there is far more at stake than the discrediting of Antony. His personal role was played down in subsequent celebrations: his name is scarcely mentioned, whether in Augustus' own brief record of his life's achievements in his *Res Gestae*, or in the poetic treatments of the event, by Horace, Virgil and Propertius. For the myth-making required that Actium should be

Fig. 4 Coin of Antony, 34-31 BC. Antony celebrates his 'conquest' of Armenia (ANTONI ARMENIA DEVICTA), while Cleopatra enjoys her new title of Queen of kings and of sons who are kings (REGINAE REGUM FILIORUM REGUM) after the powers granted to her and her sons by Antony over some eastern provinces. Under her bust is a ship's beak, stressing her naval power.

seen as far more than a battle between individuals for supremacy. It was a battle for Roman values, to save the Roman world from a frontal assault on its gods, its ideals, its moral fabric. The threat was not a tipsy Antony, but the evil incarnate in Cleopatra; the victory was one of Roman decency over barbarism and corruption. Antony was an (almost) innocent victim: a man unmanned, and a Roman un-Romanned.

The images which the poets conjured up emphasise the gulf between the Roman and the alien. Roman troops under orders from a woman, or, worse, her wrinkled eunuchs, and gauze canopies amid the military standards shock Horace (*Epodes* 9) – though mosquito nets were certainly needed as disease ravaged Antony's troops. When Horace celebrates the victory, with Roman religious ritual and good ancestral wine, it is because the Capitol, head and heart of Rome, has escaped ruin at the hands of a crazed Queen and a crowd of men polluted with shameful disease (*Odes* 1.37). For Virgil, Actium is the centre of the heavily symbolical vision of Roman history figured on Aeneas' shield (*Aeneid* 8.675-728). Appropriately enough, on a shield made by one god (Vulcan) and commissioned by another (Venus), it is seen as a battle of the gods, who embody the values of Roman and alien, of good and evil. Augustus goes to war with fathers (senate) and people, with domestic gods, Penates, and Great gods, and with a halo of fire playing round his temples from the star of his God-Father. Antony meets him with all the multicoloured barbarism of the Orient: there at the centre is the Queen, rattling the sistrum, ritual instrument of Isis, and summoning together a coven of Egyptian monster-gods, dog-headed Anubis barking at the civilized trio of Neptune, Venus and Minerva. Above them all stands Apollo, god of Actium, striking terror into Egyptian, Indian and Arab. West met East, with a clash of religion and culture no less violent than that of Christianity and Islam.

Apollo was so potent as a cultural and political symbol that the love-poet Propertius could hang his whole account of Actium around the god's role. It was in Phoebus Apollo's bay that the cosmic struggle took place (*Elegies* 4.6). The enemy fleet was damned in advance by the deified Romulus, Augustus blessed by Jupiter. Apollo leaves Delos to stand above Augustus' prow; he lays aside his lyre and his role as god of music and poetry, and takes up his terrible guise of the avenger of piety and purity, who with his arrows once struck plague into the camp of Agamemnon. He calls on Augustus as saviour of the world to free his country from fear. The enemies' vast hulks will not dismay him, for justice is on his side. Apollo's bow and Augustus' spear win the day, and the celebratory temple built for Phoebus on the Palatine allows the god to return to his role as the patron of poets – the temple was associated with the finest public library in Rome. As these poetic accounts move further in time from the event (Horace's poems belong to the period of the campaign, Virgil's to a decade later, and Propertius' to the decade after that), the realistic details give way to symbolism. By Propertius, the enemy is almost lost to sight. What matters is the chain of values in which Augustus is the vital link: divine blessing, Roman tradition, purity and justice, peace and high culture.

In the myth of Actium, then, Augustus fought as a saviour to save the Capitol from ruin, the Roman world from destruction, and Roman civilization and values from corruption. The unmanning of Antony was only a specimen of what threatened every Roman who came into contact with this pollution: Munatius Plancus had only just got away in time. The significance of this myth stretches far beyond the propaganda war of the 30s BC. The origin of the myth certainly lies in Octavian's attempts to achieve a united front in 32 BC, to engineer the massive demonstrations of support in the west in the form of the 'Oath of all Italy', and to legitimise his own legally questionable standing with the manifestation of 'common consent'. But after the battle was over, and after the fall of Egypt and the suicide of Antony and Cleopatra the next year, the need to discredit Antony faded. What Augustus needed to justify was not his position at Actium, but his position from then on. Why, having assembled a crusade to rid the world of the Eastern pest, and having succeeded, did his military supremacy continue unbroken? Because, the myth tells us, the threat was no ephemeral one, laid to rest with victory. It was permanent: Rome and the civilization she stood for were for ever in danger, for ever in need of a saviour.

The threat, as all Romans were aware, was not simply from outside. It came from within. Normally Roman might could stand up to any external threat, let alone from a bunch of barbarian eunuchs. It was only when the Romans damaged their own defences by civil war, by brother slaying brother, that Scythians and Parthians threatened to canter over the ruins of the Capitol. Cleopatra represents only a secondary danger: she could not be held responsible for the civil war itself. For that the Romans themselves were to blame: it was an inherited sin, the curse of Remus, who fell by the hand of his brother, Rome's founder (Horace, *Epodes* 7). Their sins had provoked the anger of the gods, seen in hailstorm and Tiber floods; and the Romans must fall to their knees and pray for one to expiate their sin, a saviour sent by Jupiter from outside, a god in the human form of Caesar (Horace, *Odes* 1.2, close to Virgil, *Georgics* 1.498ff.).

Poetic hyperbole, over the top? If so, the poet is only seeking for images to express real fears. Civil war is the ultimate terror for any society. The experience of some 20 years from Caesar's crossing of the Rubicon suggested that there was no way that the Romans could solve the problem from within, that is from within their existing structures and traditions. That is why a saviour from outside, sent as it were by the gods, was required. The effect of the civil wars was literally traumatic: in something of the way that the trauma of Hiroshima has hung over world politics to the present, so the trauma of civil war was at the heart of Roman consciousness. Poets used various images to express it. Virgil includes a group at the centre of his battle scene on the shield: iron-clad Mars, god of war, raging; the avenging spirits of the Dirae, the Furies of the underworld; Discord personified with her dress ripped apart; and the war goddess Bellona with a bloody flail. Jupiter had already prophesied at the start of the epic that Augustus would bring these forces of destruction under control: a harsh age would soften and lay war aside; the terrible gates of war would shut tight, and Fury would be locked within with its weaponry, chained with a hundred links of brass, groaning and frothing at the mouth with blood (*Aeneid* 1.290-6).

The fury envisaged by Virgil had not been eliminated: it threatened to burst its bonds, smash open the gates, and break out. The threat was real enough, and continued to hang over the Roman empire for four centuries, constantly liable to destroy the structures of security, and the constant justification for the continuation of Augustus' emergency powers by his successors. It was a terror with which they sought to come to terms in their imaginative literature. Lucan's epic *Pharsalia*, a century after Actium, returned to dwell on the horrors of civil war, to a society that tore out its own guts in self-destructive frenzy. This epic's double-edged dedication is to the emperor, Nero, whose death was to precipitate the next civil war. As Nero's tutor Seneca reminded him, he was sent by the gods on a mission of deadly urgency: the Romans were an immense crowd, full of discord, sedition and uncontrolled urges, and ever liable to erupt in a self-destructive frenzy if the yoke of imperial rule was broken; without his protection, a thousand swords were ready to spring up and destroy the Roman world (Seneca, *On Clemency* 1.1). The terror was a real one, and the function of imperial propaganda was to keep alive the awareness of the terror that justified the brutalities of imperial rule.

Chapter 2

Metamorphosis

The historian Cassius Dio opens Book 51 of his Roman history by observing that though he does not normally date events to the day, the date of Actium, 2 September, 31 BC, is important because it marks the beginning of the sole power, and therefore the reign, of the young Caesar. Dio is right. This date if any marks a turning point in Roman history: on which the 'Republic' finally and irrevocably ends, and the 'Empire' or 'Principate', the rule of *imperatores* or *principes* begins. The inhabitants of the Roman Mediterranean probably sensed the same even at the time: an old order had passed, and a new dawn had broken, even if they had little idea of what the new dawn would bring. As Augustus put it, 'after I had extinguished civil wars, by universal consent I gained control over all affairs' (*Res Gestae* 34). Their consent may not have been universally enthusiastic – though many went out of their way to advertise at least the appearance of enthusiasm; but willingly or not, they had to admit that he had won control.

Though the turning point may be precise, it marks neither the beginning nor the end of the process of transformation. Ovid, who constructed a mythological epic towards the end of Augustus' reign around the theme of Metamorphosis, of bodies changed from one form to another, understood that despite appearances, transformations are neither instantaneous nor abrupt. His metamorphoses take place gradually, sometimes gruesomely so, and the new shapes are fashioned, element by element, from the old. The beautiful girl Arachne, so skilled at spinning, becomes a spider through the gradual shrinkage of her head and body, and the transmutation of her long slender fingers into the spinning legs of a spider; in her new guise, she keeps weaving as before (*Metamorphoses* 6.140ff.). Or, in a contemporary image, one can consider how a few strokes of the pen may convert the Statue of Liberty into an image of the Police State (Fig. 5). To transform the one into the other, subtle adaptation will suffice. And if, to pursue this image, Liberty may be taken to stand for the Republic and the policewoman for the empire, Augustus' reign is the ambivalent figure between, standing for different ideals from different viewpoints.

Fig. 5 America as Liberty transformed to police state. © Peter Brookes, *The Times*.

Augustus' transformation of Rome was a long and gradual process: the full 45 years of his reign were spent discovering the consequences for Rome of the victory at Actium, experimenting and working out implications. It should not be imagined that Augustus had a blueprint, and knew in advance what sort of a system he was likely to create. On the contrary, we see him again and again forced to change his mind and reverse earlier initiatives. It may seem obvious to us that a system of imperial government, with more or less the features that were to remain constant for the next couple of centuries, would be developed. But it was not obvious to Augustus or to the Romans now looking to him for a solution. That helps to explain the paradox that he set about creating a new system by restoring the old one. From different viewpoints, we may see this 'restoration' as a devious and cynical piece of political manipulation, or as a false start that later required drastic modification.

Restoring the Republic

Actium placed the victorious leader in a dilemma. He had led the 'senate and people' of Rome to war (a staggering 700 senators crossed the seas in display of solidarity), on their urging, so he claimed, to free Rome from threat and preserve the traditions Rome stood for. He had proclaimed, more than once, that his desire was to restore normality and traditional government. The dilemma was created by his own position. Roman tradition, which he was so fervently championing, had no way of finding place for a champion. Hatred of kings was an old Roman tradition which was painfully fresh in all minds, ever since Caesar's assassins found a second Brutus symbolically to rid Rome of a second Tarquin. That there should be no concentration of power in the hands of a single citizen was a principle constantly reiterated over the last decades. The dilemma, then, was that the saviour could only save the Republic by eliminating himself.

Fig. 6 (a) Gold coin of Cossus Lentulus, c. 12 BC: the fallen Republic (RES PUB) is raised from her knees by Augustus (AUGUST). (b-c) The honours of 13 January, 27 BC; (b) oak wreath for saving the lives of citizens (OB CIVIS SERVATOS); (c) the shield of virtue, CL(ipeus) V(irtutis), awarded by senate and people and the name Augustus, awarded by SPQR.

The paradoxical solution was to do exactly that. The new order was secured by a 'restoration' of the old (Fig. 6), and that was marked by the 'stepping down' of the leader. Augustus' own account of the transaction at the end of his own *Res Gestae* remains crucial:

In my sixth and seventh consulships [28, 27 BC], after I had
extinguished civil wars, and by universal consent gained control over all affairs, I restored the *res publica* from my power
to the full discretion of the Senate and People of Rome. For this
service, by decree of the senate I received the name of Augustus, and the doorposts of my house were decked with laurels,
a civic crown was fixed above my door, and a golden shield
was set up in the Curia Julia, testifying that the award was made
by the Senate and People of Rome in recognition of my virtue,
clemency, justice and piety.

(Res Gestae 34)

The precise date of this momentous ceremony (13 January, 27 BC) is
recorded by the state calendars, which celebrated the Ides of January
henceforth as a festival: 'the Senate decreed that a garland of oak be
placed above the door of the house of Imperator Caesar Augustus
because he restored the *res publica* to the People of Rome'. Ovid too in
the extraordinary poem in which he contrives to set the calendar to verse,
marks the date:

Every province was returned to our People,
And your grandfather was called by the name of Augustus.

(Fasti 1.589f.)

Historians treat Augustus' claims with healthy scepticism. Power
resigned? Every province restored? The Senate and People now in full
control? The historian Dio knew, after more than two centuries of
imperial duplicity and 'newspeak', that what mattered was what emperors did, not what they said. Augustus, ceding to 'pressure' from a
horrified senate, 'reluctantly' agreed, albeit on a 'temporary' basis, to
take back control, if not of everything, at least of the nerve-centre of
power, the provinces in which the main armies were stationed, Gaul,
Spain, Syria and Egypt. The same meeting, Dio observes slyly, gave the
game away by voting a pay rise to the emperor's personal guard, the
Praetorians.

The cynical historian who, like Dio, or his far greater predecessor
Tacitus, despises the lies in which unaccountable autocratic power wraps
itself up, will neither acknowledge any significant difference in the
control exercised by Augustus before and after his renaming, nor will
trouble greatly over the legal formalities in which that power was
expressed. There has been argument over how his *imperium*, his legal

right to raise and command legions and order citizens around in general, was defined, whether as consular or proconsular, limited to his own provinces or universal, superior or infinite, and so on. It is plausible enough that so long as he held the consulship, as he did from 27 to 23 BC, his office gave him the requisite authority, and that when he resigned the consulship in 23 he had to be granted, probably with periodic renewals, a special proconsular *imperium*. Yet the most surprising, and perhaps the most important, point to make about this is that in the long series of public documents, from the *Res Gestae* to coins and inscriptions of his decrees and decisions, which are bedizened with his ceremonial powers and honours as ostentatiously as the ribbons on the breast of any modern dictator, no definition of his *imperium* is offered. His name, Imperator (supposedly just a personal name), said it all.

But cynical realism is not enough. The Ides of January was not just, perhaps not at all, a hollow charade. After all, if it was a show of resignation, it did not fool anyone, and it would have been disastrous had it done so. Everybody now acknowledged that the provinces of the empire were divided into two types, those of the senate and people, which had their governors appointed by lot according to tradition, and 'Caesar's provinces', governed by subordinates ('legates') of his own choice, not all of them even of senatorial rank. Nor did anybody imagine that Augustus' authority stopped short at the boundaries of his own provinces. The inhabitants of the empire continued to proclaim loudly and unambiguously their allegiance and devotion to Augustus. 'Since your divine mind, Caesar, has taken over care of all things...' wrote the architect Vitruvius, without trace of embarrassment. Or as Horace put it, 'I fear no more to die by violence while Caesar holds the earth' (*Odes* 3.14.15f.). As an exercise in deception, the 'restoration' would have been singularly implausible.

What was needed was neither a way to deceive Romans about the realities of power, nor a legal formula, but a way of incorporating the figure of the all-powerful champion into the traditional Roman set of ideals. Since there was no room for an all-powerful figure *within* the *res publica*, he placed himself *outside* it.

Ordinary and extraordinary powers

One way of seeing this is in terms of the idea of 'emergency powers'. A modern government may declare a state of emergency, allowing it to override the normal rules with emergency rules, particularly martial law. This suspends, but does not abolish, the normal constitution. This, in effect, is what Octavian, Antony and Lepidus had done when they seized control as triumvirs in 43 BC: although the normal apparatus of assemblies, senate and magistrates remained in operation, they used the state of crisis to override the system by choosing the magistrates and army commanders themselves, and by intervening as they saw fit in the administration of public finance and justice. After Actium, Octavian was left with full emergency powers – although it is not clear that anything beyond the vague 'universal consent' actually provided a legal basis for this, let alone the consulship which he held. After his return to Rome and his triumph in 29 BC, he gradually wound down the 'state of emergency', until on the Ides of January 27 he was ready to announce that the crisis had passed, and traditional government was again possible.

But his announcement was premature, as he well knew. It was necessary to make some exceptions, and to say that although 'ordinary' government had returned, certain 'extraordinary' areas still required his attention. Above all, because, despite the termination of civil war, Rome's foreign enemies still presented a menace, the legions could not be disbanded (the ultimate ideal). All were aware that legions were a political threat to the stability of the res publica, since commanders might try again to seize power for themselves: it was in everybody's interests that he should remain in command. It was therefore as a temporary measure that Augustus agreed to retain an extraordinary control. The hope must be that he establish a true and profound world peace, which would allow the emergency to pass finally.

Wars apart, it might be hoped that the res publica could now function fully. However, Augustus would be there to keep an eye on things, as a sort of guardian angel, to exercise what the Romans called a tutela or cura, a role of guardian or protector. He had saved the state in the past, and his job was to keep it safe. That was a role which could not possibly be defined or circumscribed in legal terms. The power we know to have been voted a century later to Vespasian on his accession as emperor, to do whatever he judged to be in the best interests of the Republic, goes back to the role developed by Augustus (whether or not the senate voted him the power in precisely these words). It did not mean that he had the power or responsibility to do everything (the claim made by the mad Caligula), but that he must do everything to save the state. What that might mean could only emerge with the passing of time, but there is no need even for the most cynical historian to suppose that Augustus anticipated quite how extensively area after area of public life would prove to be in need of his extraordinary 'saving' powers.

Now this way of seeing things, by creating a division between the normal and the abnormal, the ordinary operations of the Roman senate and people and the extraordinary operations of Caesar, had the effect of placing Augustus outside the norms, outside rules and constraints. It meant that he was no longer an ordinary Roman citizen. He might be a magistrate, and indeed he was to exercise many magisterial functions; but this did not explain his extraordinary role. As he put it, 'after this time, I exceeded all others in weight of authority, but had no powers greater than those who were my colleagues in any given magistracy' (*Res Gestae* 34). It wasn't his being a magistrate that made him special. His role put him beyond Roman, and therefore human, norms.

At this point the Romans could only take refuge in theological language. His role was more like that of a god than a man: a limitless power, to save human life and bring order to the world. Just as Jupiter and the other gods were vital for Rome's success, and possessed of almost incomprehensibly vast powers, yet obviously did not owe their powers to the senate and people, so Augustus' power *approximated* to the divine. His role left him shuttling between the human and the divine. Of course he was mortal, and a Roman citizen, and many of the functions he performed were human and traditionally Roman. But one could think of him as being on loan from heaven – a superman, sent down by Jupiter to help where no ordinary human aid could avail. We should be very careful not to dismiss language like this, which is pervasive in the poets of the day, as a type of rather tasteless flattery. They were struggling to give words to the inexpressible. They were attempting to articulate a relationship which had no real precedent in Roman tradition.

Honours

Much of this is already implicit in the name Augustus. We are offered enough contemporary comment on why this name was chosen to understand how a name could be felt to be adequate response to the political gesture of resigning power. Ovid elaborates: many great Romans had been given new names in recognition of their conquests, some recalling the peoples they had subjected, and others, Pompeius Magnus and Fabius Maximus, their human greatness. Only Augustus shared a name with Jupiter. 'August' was the word used of temples and sacred things; it was linked with the *auguries* by which the will of the gods was made known; and it evoked the *aug*mentation of the empire by Augustus, under whose *aus*pices they fought (*Fasti* 1.591-616). The choice of a word with superhuman connotations was an essential element of the political response. Senate and people found themselves unable to describe his power any more in ordinary legal terms, and therefore took refuge in the metaphor of divinity. The choice was inspired. 'Augustus' had rich enough connotations to make clear that the man was not like any other Roman, now or in the past; yet it did not make the false claim that he actually was a god. The canvassed alternative, Romulus, was crude by comparison; the first emperor to be a Romulus was the last.

'Augustus' came complete with a batch of other honours, equally without constitutional implications, and the more powerful in their symbolic content for their simplicity (Fig. 6). The *corona civica*, the civic crown of oak leaves, was a standard award for saving the life of a citizen in battle. It was traditionally presented by the grateful citizen saved, who would in future treat his saviour with especial reverence, as a father. Augustus had saved the lives of all of them, and senate and people in making the presentation put themselves permanently in his debt. Laurels meant victory, for ever. And the golden shield, placed beside a statue of victory in the senate house, proclaimed his virtues – not a manifesto of a government's policy, as we anachronistically read it, but a celebration by the Romans of the qualities in which Augustus' more than human power was revealed.

Rituals of honour were a characteristic feature of the new order. It is tempting to regard them as boastful statements by the ruler himself. But this misses the point of the ritual. They were part of an exchange between ruler and ruled. Because he placed himself outside the range of traditional, constitutional definition, the victor of the civil wars created the need for a new kind of language. The profusion and inventiveness of the honours loaded upon Augustus is staggering: statues, columns, triumphal arches, altars, names and titles, rituals and ceremonials. They changed the face of Rome and the patterns of public life. They, rather than any office or magistracy, were the expression of acknowledgement for the service rendered by a benefactor, who had taken upon himself the more than human role of saving the *res publica*.

But what exactly was it that he had saved? In what sense did he 'restore' the *res publica*? Did he really hand back power? In what ways did his continuing presence as 'guardian' and 'protector' compromise traditional government?

Ancestral tradition

First, the *res publica*. It is essential to get away from the notion that Rome had a fixed constitution called the Republic which Augustus failed to restore. The Romans neither had, nor even approved the idea of, a fixed constitution. What they had was a living tradition, a history of constant development and adaptation. It was this historical element which Cicero stressed in his theoretical work, *On the Republic* – unlike its model by Plato which saw the historical process as leading on from one type of constitution to another, Cicero saw a gradual accumulation of wisdom and improvement within the same tradition. The Romans would not have identified their state with a group of legal statutes. Statutes were vital (though Tacitus was to observe that the more of them there were, the worse the state of the Republic). But they worked alongside custom, *mos*, the nexus of traditions and examples, good and bad, which each generation inherited from its ancestors and used to orient its own conduct. This heritage of precedent, the *mos maiorum*, was not rigid and prescriptive, but subject to interpretation and improvement. Augustus' claim was not at all that he had set back the clock to some fictitious date in the Roman past and revived the authentic traditional constitution. On the contrary, he claimed to have placed himself within a long tradition of evolution, to have scoured the past for the best precedents to solve present problems, and to have offered to future generations a series of new solutions and new precedents for imitation (*Res Gestae* 8). When he spoke of the 'new status' the foundations of which he felt he had laid, he did not mean that he had given Rome a 'new constitution', but a new version of an old constitution which was founded on deep respect for the past, but knew of no definitive moment.

For this vision of the Roman tradition, and of the relationship of past and present, Augustus was clearly indebted to Cicero, who already in the *Philippics* had shown the way to cloak illegal power by invoking the 'safety of the state'. He also drew on a whole body of discussion from the preceding generation, including the monumental works of Terentius Varro, *On antiquities human and divine*, which explored what the true Roman traditions were. He relied on these 'antiquarian' writings for many of his revivals, some of which were frankly bogus. His vision found expression in a variety of monuments, not least his triumphal arch of 19 BC, which carried lists of all the triumphs of Roman history from the founder Romulus to his own day; and in his new forum, in which statues of the great Romans of the past were erected, 'as an example', so he himself declared, 'against which the citizens should demand that he should personally be measured, so long as he lived, and subsequently the *principes* of future generations' (Suetonius, *Augustus* 31). The same vision underpins the picture of Roman history in Virgil's *Aeneid*: Augustus is the culmination of the long line of heroes yet to be born who make Aeneas' mission worthwhile, the promised one of Jupiter's prophecy who will bring to fruition the plan preconceived in the foundation of Rome, of world-rule and universal peace and justice.

Just as it is possible to replace over the course of time the parts of a car one by one, until nothing remains of the original machine, and yet to continue to regard it as the same car, because of the historical continuity which holds together new and old, so it is reasonable to think of Augustus as 'restoring' the Republic, although substantially overhauling and replacing a good many of its parts. It is pedantry to complain that he did not restore the status quo that had existed immediately before the civil wars: he did not claim to be doing so. On the other hand, one can reasonably object that there were certain features of the Roman tradition that could not be disposed of without radically altering its nature. Some would say that Augustus made changes, particularly in the structure of power, so radical that his pose of 'restoration' is sheer hypocrisy.

Sovereignty

The most fundamental issue is that of sovereignty. Implicit in the name *res publica* (crudely: 'public business' or 'common wealth') is the sovereignty of the people, the *populus Romanus*, the body of Roman citizens. Like the typical Greek *polis*, Rome was a city-state, that is to say, a state with a legally defined body of citizens who enjoyed equal rights under its laws, and who had ultimate control over its destiny in war and peace. As in other city-states, the citizens met with considerable frequency, whether in the focus of the city, the forum, or elsewhere nearby, to vote for the election of their own annual magistrates, and to pass laws and make decisions on war and peace.

The Senate

It is a modern myth that the key characteristic of the Roman Republic was the power of the senate. A democracy Rome was not (though this was the word Greeks used to render *res publica*), at least not a democracy of the Athenian type. In many ways the powers of the ordinary citizen were severely limited, both by complex electoral arrangements which tilted the voting sharply in favour of the rich, and by traditions of social dependency, between men bound by ties of obligation, which enabled the rich to convert their economic, social and religious muscle into political influence. If Rome was compared to a Greek state, it was to Sparta not to Athens. But in undemocratic Sparta too, though it had two kings, and a council with lifelong membership, the citizen body was sovereign.

In Rome's case, we may be struck by the stranglehold which a virtually hereditary caste of a small group of families, the so-called nobility, established over high office. But a vital feature of their dominance was that it was achieved through a system of popular election. By whatever means, whether inherited ties of dependency, proof of effectiveness in the field, the acquisition of a reputation and popular support, or intrigue and outright bribery, the members of the dominant class realised their power through sharp competition for the votes of citizens. The tendency of the century of politics preceding the civil wars had not been to play down the significance of the citizen vote, but to enhance it, as members of the elite risked antagonising their peers and acting against their own class interests by promoting measures in the interests of the citizen poor. Though the *populus Romanus* may have got a raw deal out of its ruling class, the power of their rulers derived directly and tangibly from themselves.

It is therefore a distraction to focus diagnosis of the location of power under Augustus on the senate. Augustus went out of his way to 'revive' the traditional senate, carefully preserving the conventional pattern and number of magistracies, reviewing its membership and procedures, arguably improving its efficiency by the introducing of a committee to give preliminary consideration to important issues. Of course, the whole tone of the imperial senate is quite different from that of the republican one, as is most conspicuous in its new preoccupation with devising new honours for Augustus himself. But it is not clear that it had lost (or had ever possessed) any sovereign powers. Again, we tend to see a group of families, the republican 'nobility', as the losers (though in fact Augustus tended to favour and to bind to his own family by marriage alliances the few noble survivors of the civil wars); but then, a Roman could retort that this 'nobility' had no right to power in the first place. Powerful cliques were a menace to the freedom and sovereignty of the people.

But what of citizen-power under Augustus? Here was the main casualty of the civil wars. The dynasts, from Pompey and Caesar to the triumvirs including Octavian, had used their popular support with two vital sectors of the citizen body, the troops and the urban masses, to usurp the powers of the *populus*. The massive demonstrations of support from the populace excused and legitimised an interruption in the exercise of popular power. It was they, the dynasts, who distributed magistracies, to their own supporters naturally, sometimes years in advance. It was they who distributed army commands, and decided questions of peace and war. If the citizen body was left with a role, it was no more than ceremonial.

Elections

In theory, and partly in practice, Augustus restored this popular sovereignty in 27 BC. Elections, which in modern societies too are the critical test of the end of military or party dictatorship, returned: they were open, contested, and on more than one occasion led to rioting. There were problems again with bribery, a good litmus of the significance of the voter. In such circumstances, of course, Augustus felt obliged to intervene 'in the interests of the *res publica*', but otherwise he strictly limited his own influence to the support of individual candidates, at a level calculated to avoid undermining the process itself. A pledge of the sincerity of his restoration of free elections was the construction by Agrippa of a massive new voting hall on the Campus Martius, the Saepta Julia. When, as late as AD 5, the senate was seeking for suitable ways to commemorate Augustus' lamented grandsons, Gaius and Lucius, electoral procedure provided a sufficiently conspicuous occasion (some voting groups were named after them).

And yet the paradox, which accurately reflects the deep ambiguity of Augustus' role, is that the man who revived free elections also extinguished them. Properly speaking, that only happened after his death, on the accession of Tiberius in AD 14. Alleging posthumous instructions from Augustus, Tiberius arranged that in future the choice would be made within the senate, and the electorate probably found itself presented with a fixed list of candidates to return. It is interesting that Augustus could not bring himself, in his lifetime, to take this step, so symbolic of the abrogation of the popular sovereignty he had revived. But he had long since taken the measures which made the final step a formality.

Elections make no sense unless the candidates have access to the electorate. The republican nobility owed their power not to any hereditary privilege, but to their success in self-glorification: spectacular triumphs, conspicuous public monuments, lavish shows, these and many lesser gestures brought them fame and popularity. But Augustus too owed his power to popularity, and could tolerate no hint of rivalry. In the 20s BC, true, after the 'restoration', old traditions of self-glorification continued, as they had in the civil war period. But then, gradually and inexorably, Augustus choked off anything that challenged his own monopoly of glory. Triumphs, one of the most characteristically Roman of traditions, ceased after 19 BC, in future a privilege reserved for the imperial house. A whole variety of prominent people put up public monuments in the city, and with his encouragement; but only at the beginning of the reign. For a brief period, in the 'teens BC, the tradition was revived of the young senators responsible for minting coins to put their own family emblem on at least one side of the coin; within a few years that had gone, and only the faces and achievements of Augustus and his family could be seen on the currency. Shows, especially gladiatorial games, pulled the crowds: but new regulations placed strict limits on the expenditure of any impresario but the emperor, whose shows became ever more lavish.

How Augustus turned the city of Rome from a place of competition to an imperial showplace is the theme of chapter 4. One small incident, however, gives a hint of his intolerance of competition for popular support, however trivial. In the late 20s BC, an enterprising young senator, one Egnatius Rufus, during his tenure of the office of aedile, which carried responsibility for the roads and buildings of the city, saw an opportunity to make his mark by setting up a standing force of several hundred slaves as firefighters – astonishingly, though Rome was plagued by fires, there seems to have been no such force before. At the end of the year, he boasted that he handed over the city to his successor intact. On a wave of popular enthusiasm, he was elected straight into the praetorship, without the interval stipulated by law; and a couple of years later he put himself up for the consulship, well in advance of the minimum age. He refused to withdraw his candidature, and there were violent public demonstrations in his favour. Eventually, this 'gladiator', as the authorities regarded him, was arrested and executed as a conspirator. That he had any intention of challenging Augustus is highly improbable: but Augustus was too conscious that his own power came from the ability to inspire popular riots to allow any other to play the game.

The citizen, then, recovered his vote, but found it devalued. The vote, in a restored republic for which the highest priority was civil peace and avoidance of conflict, must be exercised responsibly; without bribery and abuse, without riot and disorder, without passion. Insensibly, the vote reduced itself to ceremonial: to the 'long song of assemblies' that was maintained as a visible link with the past and Roman tradition. The very use of the elections in AD 5 as an occasion for honouring dead princes of the imperial house already betrays their ceremonial function; it was a gesture repeated in AD 19 for the dead Germanicus, and in AD 23 for Drusus, after even the pretence of a real choice for the electorate had been abandoned.

Soldier and civilian

Along with the vote, the guarantee of the freedom of the citizen was his right to bear arms. From the first emergence of the city-state in the Greco-Roman world in the eighth century BC there had been a close link between the military significance of the heavily-armed soldier and his political voice. Romans voted, as they fought, in centuries, and met to do so on the Campus Martius, the Martial Field outside the city boundaries. The distinction between soldier and civilian was one of place and time, not of profession. The distinction was ritually enforced: within the city boundary, the *pomoerium*, the citizen must lay aside his arms and wear a toga, and the commander must abandon his military *imperium.* Only the triumph allowed this rule to be broken, and then only for the period of the procession.

The vast war effort of the last two centuries BC meant that this distinction was not just theory. Every citizen was obliged to serve for up to 16 annual campaigns; and with up to 20% of the citizen body in the field at any one time, the chances of avoiding the obligation were slim. Particularly in the last century of the Republic, the military significance of even the poorest citizens forced the ruling class to make vast political concessions, above all in the distribution of land to the needy, and of subsidised or free corn to the city masses.

This relationship of soldier and citizen was transformed by Augustus. His power was based on the backing of his citizen troops, and his highest political priority must be to ensure that nobody could use military power to challenge or disrupt the regime. That meant that the citizen-soldier could not remain a free agent: his loyalty must be beyond question. To ensure this, Augustus redrew the boundary between civilian and soldier. The military establishment was fixed at some 28 legions: the unpredictability of annual levies and discharges was over. The maximum obligation of 16 seasons campaigning was converted into a minimum term of unbroken service, soon raised to 20 or even 25 years. Rates of pay and discharge bounty were fixed. The crucial final step from citizen militia to professional army was taken.

Bound by an annually renewed oath of personal loyalty, the soldiers became Caesar's army. They were a group apart, and as the satirist Juvenal complained a century later, missed no opportunity of lording it over the mere civilian. Augustus did not shirk to mark the separation. When he reorganised the rules for seating at the games, soldier and civilian were required to sit apart. More strikingly, when he introduced laws to regulate marriage, soldiers were the only group not encouraged to marry: on the contrary, they were forbidden to do so. The boundaries thus redrawn, the old boundary of place could be allowed to evaporate. It was still preferable to keep men in arms outside the ritual boundary of the city, the *pomoerium* – troops in the forum were too blatant a symbol of martial law, and awoke unhappy memories of past disturbances. But public order required some police presence, and gradually throughout the reign the number of troops stationed in the capital multiplied: three cohorts under the new City Prefect, seven under the Prefect of the Firewatch, and eventually, an ominous presence on the city boundary itself, the Praetorian Guard. The triumph ceased to be the only time one could see troops in the city; indeed, the triumph ceased, for its function of marking the successful conclusion of campaign and the release of the citizenry back to civilian life had ceased to be relevant. Professionals fought on.

In the final analysis, then, Augustus deprived the citizen of his power. True, he made a great fuss about the value of citizenship. He legislated to ensure that it remained a privilege, particularly by placing limits on the freedom of masters to turn their slaves into citizens by manumission. Contemporary complaints focused on the ease of manumission for the morally undesirable (e.g. those profiting from prostitution); Augustus did little in practice to stem the flood of freedmen, but at least his laws underlined the 'dignity' of citizenship. He encouraged the wearing of the national costume of the 'Romans, masters of the world and people of the toga' (Virgil, *Aeneid*, cited by Suetonius, *Augustus* 40). His own conduct was ostentatiously 'citizenly', *civilis*, a new use of the word to mark one who acted 'as if' he was a citizen in a society of citizens. But the ultimate test of citizenship, and of the freedom citizenship guarantees, is whether the citizens have a real political choice. In Augustus' metamorphosed city-state, they ended up, just as they had started after Actium, by having none.

Chapter 3
Palace and Court

Ovid, for whom the comparison of Augustus to Jupiter is a favourite theme, takes the opportunity of the standard Council of the Gods at the opening of his epic *Metamorphoses* to embark on an elaborate comparison between the abode of the Gods and the Palatine in Rome:

> There is a heavenly pathway, clear in a cloudless sky,
> Its name, the Milky Way, reflects what meets the eye.
> The Thunderer's regal mansion lies upon this road;
> To right and left each noble god has set his own abode,
> Their halls, through doors unclosing, open upon the street.
> The humble folk live elsewhere; the glorious and the great,
> The classy gods have made it their own exclusive seat.
> This place – if I may use my words a touch audaciously –
> I would not shrink to designate the Palace of the sky.
>   (Ovid, *Metamorphoses* 1.168-76)

Ovid here allows us to recapture a picture of the Palatine hill, no longer visible on the ground, dating to the days before the brick-faced concrete and ponderous ostentation of Domitian's palace took over the whole hill, leaving only fragments of earlier phases lodged in its foundations. Augustus' Palatine is still a residential quarter for the nobility as it had been under the Republic. The latest excavations at the foot of the hill confirm the presence of houses of the type Ovid describes, built around central reception halls, *atria*, that traditionally stood open to the street all day to allow easy access to clients and other callers. Their basic construction remained unchanged between 600 BC and Augustus' day. Augustus himself is seen taking his place among the *atria* of the nobility, superior to, but not different in nature from the rest of the Olympic Pantheon.

This image tells us a lot about Augustus' relationships with the traditional ruling class of Rome. It gives quite the wrong impression to say that he usurped the power of the republican nobility, suppressing the old families of the Republic, and promoting in their place a generation

25

of 'new men', supporters of modest origins. That is what he *might* have done had he wished to destroy the old Rome. But as restorer of the Republic he took care to preserve and respect the old families, allying them to his side. Rather than destroying them, he transformed them: from independent agencies, with their power rooted in popular support, to his own courtiers.

The house of Augustus

The Palatine, both because of its immediate access to the Forum, and because of its exalted associations as the hill where Romulus planted the original nucleus of the city, was always the prime site for the politically ambitious. The vicious battle between the neighbours Cicero and Clodius in the 50s (Clodius demolished his enemy's house, and tried to turn it into a shrine) showed how much symbolic importance was attached to the location. Augustus, even if his family came from Velitrae in the Alban hills, was born on the Palatine while his father was making a senatorial career. Naturally he fixed his later residence there, taking over the house of Cicero's rival Hortensius, who made a fortune from his career at the bar, and enjoyed a life of luxury.

But what struck later visitors about the house of Augustus was its modesty. As his biographer Suetonius describes it (ch. 72), the house wasn't particularly big or fancily decorated – the rooms had no marble veneer or fine pavements. While many of the rich changed bedrooms with the seasons, he slept in the same room for 40 years. Of course, the gross luxury of successors like Caligula and Nero made it tempting to exaggerate the picture of the simple Augustus; but the fragments of what must be part of his house that have been exposed in recent years (Fig. 7) tend to bear out this picture. For an impression of a luxurious house of the day, we do better to turn to the villa on the far bank of the Tiber with its lovely wallpaintings that possibly belonged to Agrippa, the 'Villa Farnesina'.

In scale, Augustus' house was certainly not comparable to the sort of 'palace' which Nero and later emperors made for themselves. He owned more property than anyone else on the Palatine (and acquired more and more through his reign) but he kept these as a string of independent households, for different branches of his ramifying family. But he was adept at finding other ways of marking his abode as that of the human equivalent to the King of Heaven.

There was position. He occupied the summit of the hill, and his next-door neighbour happened to be Romulus – a hut implausibly identified

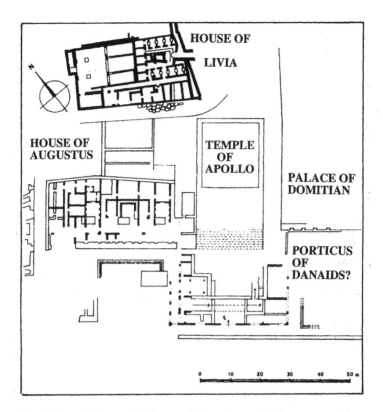

Fig. 7 Plan of the so-called house of Augustus on Palatine, preserved in a fragmentary state under later palace buildings. The portico of the Danaids and libraries must have been in front of the temple of Apollo, to the right (and left?). The so-called house of Livia must also be part of Augustus' house.

as the original one of the founder was religiously preserved there. Then there was his front door, marked out from 27 BC by the extraordinary honour of a pair of laurels and an oak wreath (Fig. 8a). But above all, he used the gods to produce a novel confusion of private and public, human and divine.

The new temple of Apollo, a thank-offering to the god who gave victory at Actium, was dedicated in 28 BC. The poets each celebrated it: Horace modestly praying to the new god not for wealth but a long life of health (on a vegetarian diet) and music (*Odes* 1.31); Virgil depicting the temple as the fulfilment of a vow by Aeneas to the Sibyl of Cumae (*Aeneid* 6.69-76); Ovid cheekily suggesting that it was a fine place to pick up a pretty girl (*Art of Love* 1.73-4). Propertius gives the most loving description: of the 'golden' colonnade of the surrounding portico with its columns of African marble and its series of statues of the daughters of Danaus (the ones who paid for the murder of their husbands by fetching water for eternity in sieves), the beauteous statue of the beauteous god (Fig. 8b), the bronze cows of Myron, and the bright white temple (*Elegies* 2.31). Not the least attraction for the poets was the addition of the best library of Greek and Latin literature in Rome.

(a) (b)

Fig. 8 (a) Coin of Caninius Gallus (12 BC) showing front door of Augustus' house with laurels on either side and oak wreath above; (b) coin of Antistius Vetus (16 BC) showing statue of Actian Apollo (APOLLINI ACTIO) holding a lyre and sacrificing. It stands on a platform decorated with ships' rostra and anchors (cf. Fig. 3).

The temple and its portico of Danaids were much visited. It was a place where Augustus received foreign embassies and summoned meetings of the senate. His house (unless the excavators have confused it with the portico itself) was so closely linked to Apollo's precinct by a system of ramps that gave direct access from house to temple that the sanctuary must be regarded as part of the palace complex (cf. Fig. 7). As if it was not enough to share a house with one god, in 12 BC when Augustus as Pontifex Maximus took over the role as chief priest, he declared his whole house public property in order to be able to move the cult of Vesta into his house. Any private modesty, then, was fully compensated for by religious solemnity.

The nobility

What of his noble neighbours? There is little evidence that they sat there grinding their teeth and plotting to throw out this newcomer and restore the *real* Republic. Augustus made a virtue of forgiving his old opponents (*clementia*): the policy was essential if he was to rule by consent. Lucius Domitius Ahenobarbus was one of Caesar's bitterest enemies, fighting him for Gaul in 49, and falling in battle against him at Pharsalus. Lucius' son Gnaeus also fought for Pompey, and later for the liberators against the triumvirs. He eventually joined Antony against Octavian, and changed sides for the last time too late, dying within a few days of the battle of Actium. But Lucius, son of Gnaeus, despite his family's consistent opposition to the Caesars, was welcomed into the bosom of Augustus' family: married to the emperor's niece Antonia, he held high office, commanded armies in Germany, and became the grandfather of an emperor, Nero. Absorption, not extinction, was the doom of the nobles.

Augustus was no enemy to blue blood. In 29 BC he received the power to add to the depleted numbers of families with patrician status. In his reign patricians, new and old, enjoyed accelerated promotion in public life. Doubtless their role was more decorative then powerful, but reminders of the past played a vital role in the new order, and it mattered to him to be surrounded by scions of the heroes of yesteryear.

There was opposition to Augustus, but not an opposition led by the old families. A young patrician, Cornelius Cinna Magnus, is said to have formed a plot, only to receive a long lecture from Augustus and later promotion to the consulship. There were individuals who loathed Augustus, and his life was always at risk – a Greek philosopher friend tried to warn him of the danger by having himself carried into Augustus' presence in a closed sedan, and leaping out brandishing a sword. But the threat was never from an organised 'party of opposition', or 'senatorial opposition': such things belong to the world of parliamentary democracy. There was a serious conspiracy in 22 BC, for which two senators, Licinius Murena and Fannius Caepio, met their end. But the idea that they were giving voice to a widespread senatorial opposition to Augustus' constitutional powers is a modern construction.

The real threats to a military dictatorship come from inside. Those within the ruling group itself, on whose support and trust the dictator relies, are in the best position to stage a coup, a palace revolution. Those to whom Augustus was most vindictive were not old enemies, but close friends whom he felt to have betrayed him. Salvidienus Rufus, a nobody whom he promoted to high command in the civil wars, was declared a public enemy and sent to his death for suspected plotting against him; Cornelius Gallus, poet and soldier, to whom he entrusted Egypt after Cleopatra's death, forfeited his friendship for ingratitude and was driven to suicide.

Court and patronage

Despite the 'restoration' of 27 BC, the pattern of politics after 20 years of civil war had already changed irrevocably. For the ambitious, those in pursuit of position, wealth or favourable judgement, realities not appearances were what mattered. The reality was that Augustus controlled the resources that mattered, and that his favour was the vital route to achieving them. Patronage had always oiled the wheels of Roman politics. The picture of nobles entering the political fray supported by armies of humble clients is too crude to help us much; the true picture is more confused, of an intricate network of favours exchanged, notes of recommendation, good turns, leg-ups, back scratching, palm greasing.... The victory at Actium at once put the victor at the centre of all webs of patronage and intrigue; and however much he denied his own control, so long as he refused to allow others independent power bases in popular citizen support and military triumph, the ambitious must necessarily look towards him – and his friends and the friends of his friends.

That is what the imperial court was about. Senators and nobles became not his victims, but his courtiers. Behind the social life, the exchange of courtesies, the dinner parties and entertainments – and Augustus took care to sustain the egalitarian 'citizenly' social manners of the Republic, and repress the fawning of an oriental court – lay the urgent pursuit of advantage and advancement. Whether openly or covertly, the key political and military appointments were made at court.

Even after the 'restoration' of 27 BC, an enormous number of appointments remained formally in the hands of Augustus. 'Caesar's' provinces (i.e. the relatively new conquests, Gaul, Spain, the Rhine and Danubian lands, Syria and the Levant, Egypt) were governed by legates of his choice, usually of the same senatorial rank as normal governors, though in Egypt the prefect was of equestrian rank. All ranks in the army, senatorial, equestrian or below, were in his control as supreme commander. Then there came the new quasi-military prefectures in Rome itself. In addition, the finances and taxes of his provinces were administered by agents ('procurators') appointed by him from among his 'friends' of equestrian rank, or his freedmen. Beyond that, there was the personal estate of the emperor, swollen by the estates of civil war opponents and whole districts in the provinces; here too he appointed procurators as his agents.

The jobs in Caesar's patronage offered exceptional opportunities for political and pecuniary advancement. One of his procurators, the equestrian Publius Vitellius from Nucerla, saw all four of his sons promoted to the senate (one of them became Claudius' leading courtier, and was father to a future emperor). Publius' origins were doubtless humble, and the acerbic orator Cassius Severus was exiled for insulting men like him – he called him descendant of a freedman rag-and-bone man. There were many fortunes made in Augustus' reign, as a rash of magnificent villas testifies (the Volusii with their fabulous villa at Lucus Feroniae are a good example). Links of friendship at court were the indispensable route to such prosperity. And not only for themselves, but in order to serve adequately their own dependents looking for advancement at lower levels, men needed to secure the favour of the emperor – or of those who had his ear.

Augustus' palace staff of slaves and freedmen did not yet exert sufficient leverage to secure prominence; not till Claudius would palace freedmen parade in open pomp in the company of consuls. But the extensive group which already did exert tremendous leverage and which proved an increasing focus of intrigue throughout the reign was his own family. If Augustus became the centre of a web, they formed the first threads around the centre.

The divine household

Augustus, who owed his own rise to his somewhat remote relationship to Caesar (his mother's mother's brother), could not underestimate the power of family ties. He traded on family ties throughout his career, a traditional Roman political tactic, but one which had the effect of giving considerable prominence to his womenfolk. True, he had only one offspring, Julia, his daughter by his first marriage to Scribonia; but he used her for three dynastic alliances (to Marcellus, Agrippa and Tiberius) and she bore five children. Augustus' own second marriage of 39 BC to Livia brought the two sons of her previous marriage (Tiberius and Drusus) into the family circle. Then there was Augustus' sister Octavia, who brought a nephew, Marcellus, by her first marriage, and two nieces, both called Antonia, by her marriage to Antony. Each of these offspring was a source of further marriage alliances and further offspring, in an ever spreading network. Tiberius, Caligula, Claudius and Nero were all its products. One obvious focus for family intrigue was the issue of succession. Augustus' delicate health in combination with his exposure to assassination meant that those with an eye to the future must always bear in mind who would step into his place. But succession was only one element in the power relations of the palace. Since any member of the household, successor or not, was likely to wield some influence with the emperor, each might be cultivated in their own right. If the palace was where the rivalries of the empire, between city and city, between group and group, between individual and individual, were resolved by imperial arbitration, the members of the household were inevitably drawn into the pattern of conflict and rivalry. They did not only compete with each other to ensure that they (or their candidate) would become the next Augustus, but for influence in much more general terms, in securing favours for their own supporters. This sort of palace faction-fighting became conspicuous in the next reign, in the conflict between the 'parties' of Sejanus and Agrippina, but the pressures were building up from the start.

One way of making sense of the political development of the reign is thus to look at the evolution of different groupings within Augustus' house. At the risk of some simplification, three periods can be distinguished: an early period, before dynastic politics have become dominant, when Octavia still has some influence; a middle period, when rivalry between Livia and Julia becomes more and more intense; and a late period of the dominance of Livia.

Early years: Octavia

During the years of the triumvirate, Octavia had played an important role for her brother. At first her function was to secure the alliance between her brother and Antony (rather as the marriage of Caesar's daughter Julia to Pompey had held together their alliance). The death of her first husband, Gaius Marcellus (by whom she had borne a son) in 40 BC left her free to marry Antony. She had played the role of model wife, not only bearing two daughters, but answering his flagrant infidelity with her own ostentatious fidelity. The contrast between the faithful wife and the foreign temptress Cleopatra helped her brother to put Antony morally in the wrong. Octavia maintained the role of model mother, continuing after her divorce (in 32) to bring up both her own children, Marcellus and the two Antonias, and adding after Antony's death his son by an earlier marriage, Iullus Antonius.

Fig. 9 Gold coin of Antony, early 30s BC, showing Octavia. She wears her hair in a bun, a sign of feminine modesty.

Octavia stood in the limelight in the 30s. Her face was portrayed on the coinage, at a time when it was still a new and daring idea to put faces of living people on Roman coinage (Fig. 9). She was the first Roman woman so to appear – and points the way for imperial ladies of the future. Her prominence continued into the 20s and was reflected in the rapid promotion of her son Marcellus. Married to Augustus' daughter Julia in 25, he held the aedileship in 23 while still 19 years old. Augustus marked the distinction further by the lavishness of the games he financed for his nephew and son-in-law; the fact that the Forum was under canvas for an extended period made a particular impression.

But 23 was a year of crisis, the first of a series of dynastic crises of a type impossible to reconstruct except by conjecture because veiled in secrecy by all involved. Augustus came close to death – to be saved by the cold baths prescribed by the doctor Antonius Musa, from his name a former member of Antony's household, and thus a member of Octavia's. On the point of death (so he thought) Augustus handed his signet ring to Agrippa and the state papers to his fellow consul. Whether or not one could think of a successor to a position so elusively defined as Augustus', it seemed that Agrippa rather than Marcellus was favoured. People talked, and Augustus (now recovered) offered to read his will – to prove what? Marcellus must have been one of its main beneficiaries. Agrippa promptly left for the east on state business. The move may have been to defuse tension in Augustus' household, though who was upset with whom we can only guess.

The death of Marcellus later in the same year, despite Musa's administration of the same cold bath treatment, put an end to the crisis, but not the gossip. We are asking too much if we demand to know what *really* happened – did Livia, as some claimed, induce Musa to poison Marcellus? Even if we were flies on the palace wall, we could not be sure what was going on in each mind. Nor could contemporaries do more than guess. But the interesting point to observe is the way they guessed and gossiped. Such crises have the effect of taking the lid off palace politics and letting one peep briefly in; and what you see is not a straightforward and unambiguous truth, but a bees' hive of rumour and intrigue, of people trying to second-guess the emperor and each other, to obscure their own motives and expose those of others. What else could be expected in the household of one whose power was a tissue of denials and motives obscured?

There were many lessons for Augustus in the episode. First, he learnt the importance of defusing rivalries and tensions within his own home. The prompt marriage of his daughter, Marcellus' widow, to Agrippa had the effect of defusing one potential tension. Secondly, he learnt that there must be a more effective way of marking, and transmitting, supreme power. It was now that 'tribunician power' was invented as the supreme imperial distinction; five years later, he shared this power with Agrippa, and subsequently with his actual successor Tiberius.

Finally he learnt the depth of the popular emotion surrounding the members of his family that could be drawn upon. Marcellus was buried with much ceremony in the new Mausoleum; later, a new theatre was dedicated in his memory. But the most powerful surviving commemoration is in poetry. The central moment of the *Aeneid*, the vital turning point between the heroic past and the conception of the new Rome, is the vision presented to Aeneas in the underworld of the souls of the future heroes of Rome (6.756-886). There was an obvious shape to this pageant, running from Aeneas' descendants through Romulus to the great names of historic Rome, and a grand culmination in Augustus, the promised one, who would restore the golden age and spread Roman rule to the ends of the earth. But Virgil shunned the obvious. The climax comes soon after the beginning: the promised Augustus follows soon after Romulus. The ensuing list of heroes must then prepare us for a further climax, one possibly even greater than Augustus. It is at this point (860ff.) that Aeneas sees the handsome young man in shining arms, with a crowd of companions around him (those companions are what a court is all about). The black shadow over his head, the tears in the eyes of Anchises, the memories of the funeral on the Campus Martius, the unfulfilled promise of the greatest of all heroes, lead to a climax which involves every reader in a sense of loss and emptiness:

You will be Marcellus. Come scatter lilies from full hands;
I shall strew purple flowers and heap a grandson's soul
With these slight offerings at least, and the futility
Of final offices.

(883-6)

To report that Octavia, on hearing these lines, broke down in grief, seems unbearably banal. A mother might grieve without being told that her son's death was the climactic tragedy of Roman fate. Indeed, we are told that Octavia was so shattered by her loss that she withdrew from court life, living in isolation till her death a decade later.

What is so remarkable is the way that a young member of the household could be used as the focus of such intense public emotion. Augustus was to take the elevation of his grandsons Gaius and Lucius far further than that of Marcellus, and the public expressions of grief on their deaths are far more extravagant. But it takes a Virgil to persuade us that behind extravagant words and gestures might be real feelings.

The middle years: Julia and Livia

The dynasticism of the early years was tentative; only in the orgy of grief at Marcellus' death does it become explicit. Augustus found substitutes for Marcellus from two quarters, his wife and his daughter. Livia's two children, Tiberius and Drusus, were step-children of the right age to do what Marcellus would have done. It was the 22-year-old Tiberius who received the return of legionary standards by the Parthians in 20 BC, a diplomatic manoeuvre which Augustus chose to elevate to the status of the emblematic triumph of his reign. Tiberius and Drusus went on to conduct one of the most successful campaigns of conquest in Roman history, crushing in a pincer movement the Alpine valleys from Switzerland to Austria (16-13 BC), the Rhineland and Germany as far as the Elbe (13-9), and the lands south of the Danube from Austria to Albania (13-6). By AD 6 Tiberius stood on the brink of a sweep north of the Danube into central eastern Europe, only to be frustrated by risings behind the frontier.

Livia's sons were not deprived of recognition, but what is striking here is how their glory was strictly subordinated to that of Augustus. He held in theory the 'auspices' of supreme command; and in practice the northern campaigns show central co-ordination and long-term planning, probably the first campaigns in Roman history to do so. But the result was that Tiberius and Drusus won laurels, quite literally, for their stepfather.

The cuirassed statue of Augustus, found at what may have been a villa belonging to Livia in the suburbs of Rome at Prima Porta (Fig. 10), elevates Tiberius' recovery of the Parthian standards to an event of cosmic significance. The figure of the young man in uniform facing a baggy-trousered Parthian king is framed by symbolic references: above we see the mantle of the Heavens, below the embodiment of the fruitful Earth with her horn of plenty; to the left Apollo, the god of Augustus'

Fig. 10 Marble statue of Augustus from Prima Porta (detail). Augustus is represented as conqueror; the breastplate shows his stepson Tiberius receiving back a standard from a Parthian.

Golden Age, shown above as the sun god, and below as the culture god with his lyre; and to the right his sister Diana, goddess of womanly purity, above as moon goddess and below as chaste huntress on a stag. Just as the loss of Roman standards to the Parthians could be taken to symbolise the folly and chaos of civil wars, their recovery marked the reversal of that era, the end of sin and strife, the return of order, purity and plenty. Tiberius enjoys the place of honour, the role of the promised one, the young man who will bring in the new age: but only in the small print – the conqueror is Augustus.

The German conquests, of far greater lasting importance than the Parthian 'victory', were suitably celebrated, including a triumph, the first since Balbus' of 19, in 7 BC. The challenge was to give Tiberius and his brother credit without obscuring the ultimate responsibility of Augustus himself. Horace several years earlier had produced a victory ode, on the model of Pindar, in which he turned to a divine metaphor to express this joint responsibility (*Odes* 4.4). The brothers were like the trusty eagle of Jupiter, learning to spread their wings and sharpen their claws on the Alpine tribes: it was a triumph not just for good breeding, but for education, for the value of an upbringing under the paternal eye of Augustus. That image of Jupiter and his eagle recurs on one of the finest of all cameos, the Gemma Augustea (Fig. 11). Probably cut at the end of the reign, it shows Augustus in the classic pose of the king of the gods, enthroned with sceptre, alongside the goddess Roma. At his feet is his eagle; and to one side his human eagle, Tiberius, descends triumphant from his chariot. Below, the barbarian captives dragged by the hair indicate the service Tiberius has done for Augustus. It is Augustus' lucky sign, the Capricorn, seen above his head, not Tiberius', which brings Rome success.

Ceremonies, poems and monuments (there will have been others, now lost, which the Gemma Augustea reflects) show Augustus cautiously building up the public image of his stepsons (while underlining his own superiority). But from the first the treatment of his own blood was different. Julia, married to Agrippa in 21, swiftly bore two sons, Gaius (in 20) and Lucius (in 18). Augustus adopted them in 17, though their father was still alive, a standard Roman way of creating heirs to one's name and fortune. They thus acquired the name of Julius Caesar – Gaius had exactly the combination of names of the dictator, his grandfather by adoption. Within a few years, their heads were to be seen on the coinage, on either side of their mother's: they were the first children depicted on Roman coinage (Fig. 12). As the boys entered their teens, Augustus invented a new distinction. They were made *Principes*

Fig. 11 Gemma Augustea. The cameo shows Augustus as Jupiter, crowned by the World, beside Rome; note his astral sign of Capricorn above his head. He holds the augur's crook (*lituus*) to indicate his power of taking auspices as supreme commander. Tiberius descends from a triumphal chariot. Captives below include a German and a Gallic Celt (with torque).

Iuventutis: as he was Princeps of adult citizens, they were leaders of the young. So they are shown on the coinage with the shields and spears of the young warriors who exercised on the Campus Martius, and participated in the 'traditional' tournament revived by Augustus, the Lusus Troiae (Fig. 13a). Contrast these images with that of Tiberius and Drusus bringing their stepfather the laurels of victory (Fig. 13b): they are subordinated to Augustus, while Gaius and Lucius are elevated by novel honours.

We see Augustus in the middle years of his reign making heavy use of his family for military command and promoting the image of the dynasty. The potential for conflict, however, is equally clear; and though many of the details must remain obscure, the formation of factions within the palace of sharply divided loyalties seems likely. There were many who served under Tiberius on campaign who looked to him for advancement, like the stolidly loyal Velleius Paterculus, who wrote a panegyrical history in his reign. These will not have shared the general enthusiasm for Gaius and Lucius.

Fig. 12 Coins of C. Marius, c. 13 BC. (a) Busts of Julia between her sons Gaius and Lucius; (b) Julia as the goddess Diana.

Fig. 13 (a) Gaius and Lucius Caesar as *principes iuventutis*, leaders of the youth, wearing togas but with silver shields and spears. This new honour involved leading a parade of young men on the Campus Martius; (b) Tiberius and Drusus present the laurels of victory to the seated Augustus. IMP X marks the tenth 'acclamation' by the troops of Augustus as victorious general, this one for the successes of Tiberius and Drusus in 15 BC.

Agrippa died in 12 BC; and the prompt remarriage of the twice-widowed Julia to Tiberius was an explicit ploy to unite the two branches of the family, Livia's sons with Julia's. It failed. Drusus died in 9, and Tiberius was elevated to a position like that of Agrippa, sharing the tribunician power with Augustus from 6 BC. Yet in the next year Tiberius left, against Augustus' will, for an extended stay in Rhodes. At the games there had been an extraordinary demonstration in favour of Gaius, demanding a premature consulship; shortly afterwards he was formally 'destined' to hold office in five years time, some 22 years ahead of the standard minimum legal age. Although Tiberius veiled his motives in a cloud of excuses, he could not conceal his incompatibility either with Julia or with Gaius and Lucius. Tiberius' departure succeeded in exposing precisely the tensions within the household Augustus most wanted to suppress, and set the fuse for a far worse explosion.

In 2 BC, a year in which Augustus took the consulship, dedicated the temple of Mars in his new Forum, and was acclaimed father of his country, *Pater Patriae*, he discovered that his daughter had been leading a scandalous life of debauchery and adultery. She had, allegedly, cavorted with a drunken party of lovers through the Forum, polluting the very Rostra from which he had promulgated new laws to enforce the sanctity of the family. In fury, he reported the full story to the senate; and invoking the full vigour of the law, banned his own daughter permanently to the small island of Pandateria, and exiled or executed her lovers. His anger was never softened, and she was left in exile despite popular demonstrations in her favour.

We would all like to be able to get behind the scenes in this row. Was Julia, mother of five and in her mid-30s, really a byword for lechery? How could she get away with it so long among the gossips of Rome without her father knowing? Did some sort of darker conspiracy lurk behind the accusations of immorality? Did Augustus act on that belief? No ingenuity can produce evidence with which to answer such questions, and we can only exercise our own skills of divination as palace-watchers.

There should be no doubt that the moral element of the scandal was crucial. Moral reform stood at the heart of Augustus' new Rome, and his own family was offered as a model of morality. The scandal gave deep embarrassment and real damage to the regime. Whether or not Julia was guilty of adultery, her father evidently believed her so. Nor is it easy to see what Julia had to gain from forming a conspiracy. With her two sons already publicly fêted as princes and heirs, and Tiberius sulking in Rhodes, her influence within the palace was at its peak.

A more plausible finger of suspicion points at Livia. The scandal destroyed Julia. It may have been intended to destroy her sons in addition, and to lead to the rehabilitation of Tiberius. It is not easy to see who in the palace apart from Livia enjoyed sufficient intimacy with Augustus to tell him of his own daughter's adulteries. Julia may well have been guilty: but to tell her father was in the circumstances purest malice. However, if the real conspiracy was Livia's, it only partly worked. Pitiless though Augustus was towards his daughter, his adopted sons remained the blue-eyed boys. Gaius, having held the consulship at 19, a record only equalled by Augustus himself, proceeded out to the east to a career of conquest – and an untimely death.

The last years: Livia triumphant

In Roman popular imagination, stepmothers were malicious creatures, intent on destroying their innocent charges by the metaphorical poison they poured into their husbands' ears and by the literal poison they administered in their food. Since Livia actually succeeded in getting her son to the throne, it was predictable that Romans should cast her in the role of the wicked stepmother. Whether or not the deaths of Lucius, at Marseilles in AD 2, and of Gaius, fatally wounded in Armenia in AD 4, owed anything to her machinations, the unspoken assumption of the day was that she was a skilful machinator. 'Ulysses in petticoats' was what her great-grandson Caligula called her.

Augustus, even if deprived by 'bitter fate' (so his will started) of heirs of his own blood, could see the effectiveness of his own manipulation of popular opinion. The effusive manifestations of public grief at the death of the princes suggest the potential perpetuation of his own relationship with the Roman people, as a saviour by popular demand rather than a ruler reliant on armed force. Public mourning in Rome was reflected town by town through the empire as at the colony of Pisa, which grieved ostentatiously over the loss of Gaius, 'already designated Princeps, most just and most like his father in virtues'.

After Tiberius' return from Rhodes (in AD 2) and his subsequent restoration to favour and renewed tribunician power (AD 4), the interests at court of his friends and supporters ought to have been irresistible. Yet intrigue lost none of its viciousness, and the sheer inability of Augustus (and Tiberius after him) to control internecine feuding within the household should give us an indication of how strong the currents of palace factionalism were. The next victim was Agrippa's posthumous son, disgraced in AD 6 not for any specific misdemeanour, but for his obstinate temperament. After him, in AD 8, a second Julia fell. Like her mother she was accused of adultery. It may be that she and a group of her mother's old supporters were plotting to bring back her mother from exile and reinstate Agrippa Postumus in Tiberius' place. But it may also be that the intense insecurity of court life made the dominant faction intolerant of the faintest whiff of rivalry, and overanxious to stamp out the survivors of the defeated side. In this game, Augustus was helplessly manipulated, and heartbroken: he spoke of his daughter, granddaughter and grandson as his 'three ulcers'.

Palace politics must remain obscure, penetrated only by conjecture. But this does not mean that their importance was slight, and limited to the palace. As the struggle within the palace became grimmer, so the whole regime became more intolerant of rivalry or questioning. It is to this late part of the reign that the multiplication of armed men within the walls of Rome belongs. It is also the period when free speech comes under attack. And a poet, Ovid, was relegated for an 'error' which he dared not specify (what sort of regime punishes men for crimes that cannot even be spoken?) and for an immoral poem. That Ovid was part of anything that can sensibly be called an 'opposition' to Augustus is not likely; who, after 40 years, could benefit from displacing a dying ruler? But he may well have had the wrong friends at court. His *Art of Love*, published at the turn of the era, apart from sailing close to the wind, happens to praise Gaius not Tiberius.

Whatever the truth of that, it is clear that by the end of the reign the focus of political intrigue had shifted decisively, from the open forum where the restoration of 27 BC should have secured it, to the circles of contacts which spread out from the ruler's private household.

Chapter 4
Golden Rome

Rome was a phenomenon among ancient cities. 'The city which they call Rome', says the shepherd hero of Virgil's pastoral poems, 'I foolishly thought was like our market town.... But she holds her head high above others, as high as cypresses among shrubs.' (Virgil, *Eclogues* 1.20ff.). By the age of Augustus, its population already far outran any rival, vast, fluctuating and uncounted – we can only guess at a figure of around a million souls. It was also exceptional in its heterogeneity: a cosmopolitan crowd of different peoples and cultures, brought forcibly by slavery, or attracted by need and ambition to this exceptional centre of wealth and power.

> Come, look at this crowd, which all the buildings of the vast city can scarcely house: the great majority of them have left their birthplaces behind them. From their towns and colonies, indeed from the whole world they have flooded together. Their reasons for coming are various: ambition, official missions, diplomatic duties; luxury (this spot offers a wealth of opportunities for vices); the desire for higher education, or the shows; ties of friendship, or the wide openings for display of virtue and industry. All's for sale, from speaking skills to bodies. There's not a human type that has not converged on a city which sets an equal premium on virtues and vices.
>
> (Seneca, *On Tranquillity* 2)

As the centre of what was supposed to be a stable empire, Rome was alarmingly volatile. It was essential, if Augustus was to guarantee the peace and order of the empire, that he stabilise this volatile centre. At the same time, if he could harness its potential for explosion, it could become a potent weapon for his own protection. There was no need for fears that the capital would be moved to Alexandria, let alone Troy (Horace, *Odes* 3.3). It was the ideal showplace of rule, and expression of imperial power. Augustus, then, had a double challenge: to bring the population under control, and to turn the capital into an architectural showplace.

Controlling Rome

When revolutionaries in the late Republic wanted to raise a mob, they would go round the shops, enlisting shopkeepers and craftsmen (*tabernarii* and *opifices*); around the neighbourhoods (*vici*), where neighbours might gather together to make offerings at street-corner shrines; and around the trade associations (*collegia*) in which fellow craftsmen gathered as much for social as for economic purposes, to eat and worship together, and to contribute to common burial funds. Thousands of gravestones of such craftsmen survive from Rome, with trades ranging from the common (smiths, butchers, bakers, fullers, porters, seamstresses, midwives) to the exotic (bird-fatteners, gold spinners, makers of eyes for statues, pluckers of underarm hair). One very striking fact about them, at all periods from the late Republic into the late Empire, is that the majority are slaves or ex-slaves, many or most of them first-generation arrivals from all over, and outside, the Roman world. As such, they were often treated by the upper classes with contempt; and yet the ex-slave *liberti* were citizens and had the vote. The voice of the city *plebs* could sometimes be confused with that of the *populus Romanus*, the citizen body.

There was a strong element of the populist revolutionary in Augustus' background. From Caesar he had inherited a strong following among the city masses, which he at once consolidated with a distribution of cash. He continued to cultivate them throughout his reign. His *Res Gestae* (ch. 15) lists six occasions between 29 and 2 BC when he distributed cash or corn to each of quarter of a million or more men. In addition, he entertained them: eight gladiatorial shows involving 10,000 men, 30 athletic or other games, 26 beast shows in which 3,500 animals were slaughtered – distasteful though the statistics of bloodshed may be, they give an idea of the colossal resources pumped into keeping what a later emperor called 'my little flock' happy.

His role was that of the 'champion of the people', associated in recent experience with the office of tribune of the people. He took over some of the functions of a tribune the year after Actium, but this aspect became prominent in 23 BC. Recovering from a near-fatal illness, he resigned the consulship which he had held for the last eight years (a record) and accepted instead the powers of a tribune. This *tribunicia potestas*, renewed annually, was of limited importance in legal terms (the tribunate was a junior magistracy) but of enormous importance symbolically. It was what Tacitus calls 'the title of supreme power', what distinguished an emperor from a citizen. It evoked the fail-safe role he had taken on: not to govern, but to step in to protect the Roman people in crisis.

That did not prevent further massive demonstrations the next year in the crisis caused by a grain shortage. Twice Augustus was begged to take on the role of dictator. He appeared before the people with tears in his eyes and tore apart his toga as a symbol of grief, begging to be spared the office which had proved Caesar's undoing. Instead he took on responsibility for the grain supply. This was far from being the last riot of the reign. Famine, fires and floods were a constant menace in a grossly overcrowded city, and time and again they triggered rioting. Well handled, popular riots could strengthen his hand; out of control they could bring the regime down. Games and handouts were not enough.

Getting on top of these problems required not just cash and organisation, but imagination and experiment. Augustus continued to tussle with the problems throughout his reign and one can observe a pattern of development, away from the 'hands off' approach of the early period to a much tougher interventionism by the end. The measures against fire are a good example. We have seen the way that Egnatius Rufus was able to mobilise popularity by his creation of a fire brigade. It shows up how astonishingly inadequate were traditional arrangements, which left magistrates to run the city without the backup of services which a modern city of a million would take for granted – fire brigade, police, refuse collection and so on. But Augustus' unwillingness to intervene at this period (the same as that of his tearful refusal of the dictatorship) is seen in his response to Egnatius: he took over Egnatius' band of slaves as state property, and instructed the aediles to use them to control fires in future.

It didn't work, or not well enough. After further major fires in 16, 14, 12 and 7 BC, a more elaborate organisation was set up: Rome was divided into a number of regions, and seven separate local fire stations were put under the command of seven separate magistrates (aediles and tribunes). But the command structure was inadequate, and the fires continued to blaze. At last, in AD 6, a paramilitary force of freedmen 7,000 strong was instituted, under the command of an army officer with the rank of Prefect, reporting directly to the emperor, fully equipped with axes and buckets, and the legal right to enter households and summarily try any householder found without firefighting equipment installed. This brigade, the *vigiles*, though not always, as Nero found to his cost, effective, remained in place for four centuries, and its name is still remembered in the *Vigili* of modern Rome (it was an officer of the *Vigili* who wrote a history of the imperial brigade in 1898).

What is typical about this pattern is the movement away from the traditions of the city-state, which relied essentially on popular self-help, run by a small group of popularly elected magistrates, enjoying high social respect, but with little force or manpower at their disposal, to a militaristic solution, disposing of considerable force and personnel, and run by a non-elected officer of lower social grade (the Prefect was an equestrian, a rank below the senatorial aediles), but with the authority of the emperor behind him.

We see something similar with the grain supply. Food shortages were the commonest cause of riot in most cities down to recent times, and the sheer organisational problems of keeping a million mouths supplied were formidable. After the riots of 22 BC Augustus, still relying on traditional institutions, set up a senatorial board in charge of distributing grain. But it proved not enough to supervise the distribution of a free ration to citizens: active measures were required to secure the provision of grain in the first place. By AD 8 this was reorganised under a military Prefect with staff. The first appointee, one Turranius, served for 40 years, and sailed far and wide in execution of his duties – he reported sighting a mermaid off Cadiz. But it was not until the emperor Claudius, doubtless on Turranius' advice, constructed an artificial harbour at the mouth of the Tiber, turning Ostia into the centre of the Mediterranean grain trade, that the problem was brought under control.

Police

Controlling Rome meant ultimately the deployment of force. It seems odd to us that republican Rome had no police: but it went against the ideology of the city-state for the citizen to be subject to armed violence in his own city. Augustus' first attempt to create a police chief or City Prefect, 'to control the servile elements in the population and contain disorder', collapsed: Messala Corvinus resigned his post within a few days, declaring his powers 'uncitizenly'. But by the end of the reign, the 3,000 men of the Urban Cohorts were a permanent institution, under the command of a senior senator with the power to administer summary justice.

The Praetorian Guard, which was rapidly to become the most blatant symbol of the military force that sustained imperial power, was also a tentative development. As army commander (in archaic terms, 'praetor', and headquarters was still called the 'praetorium') Augustus must always have had a detachment of 'praetorians' at his side. They received, we have seen, a pay-rise when Augustus 'resigned' in 27 BC. But their function was transformed from guarding to policing. As the only troops stationed in Italy, Augustus found them convenient for suppressing brigandage and kidnapping. They were also useful for crowd-control within the city. Their presence at the games became as vital as that of the police in a modern football stadium. But this emergence of a police function was gradual: only in 2 BC were they given a separate command structure with the appointment of two Praetorian Prefects (equestrian officers like the Fire Prefect and Grain Prefect), and only after Augustus' death did the prefect Sejanus construct his great barracks on the city boundary, which thereafter stood as the most vivid reminder of the force that underpinned imperial power.

Regions and neighbourhoods

Force was by no means Augustus' only instrument of control. One of his most lasting changes was the reorganisation of the city into regions which we have met in the context of fire control. Dividing a city into 14 regions may not sound like a dramatic innovation. But in an unostentatious way, it had its own importance. Large conurbations need a substructure, of wards, parishes, neighbourhoods or whatever, in order to preserve the sort of 'face to face' human unit which saves a city from becoming a pathless jungle. In the remote past, Rome had been divided into four urban tribes; but these tribes had long since ceased to have any bearing on patterns of residence. Worse, the city lacked any organisation or identity as a city. Its organs of government (senate and assemblies), and its local magistrates, had become hopelessly confused with those of a world empire. There were considerable attractions in allowing senate and magistrates to focus on empire-wide problems, and to cope with specifically urban ones at a much humbler local level.

The 14 divisions of Rome, *Regiones*, instituted by Augustus in 7 BC still survive today technically in modern Rome as 'Rioni' (Fig. 14). They were a level of official organisation that mediated between the high level running of the state, and the social realities of the neighbourhood, the *vicus*. So it was at regional level that the fire service was organised, and also, to judge by a list that survives from the fourth century, that local registers of property were kept – the preserved lists enumerate region by region the numbers not only of public buildings, houses and apartment blocks, but grain silos, water tanks, baths, bakeries, public latrines and brothels. The fact that the central regions including the main monumental complexes like the Forum have as many houses, flats,

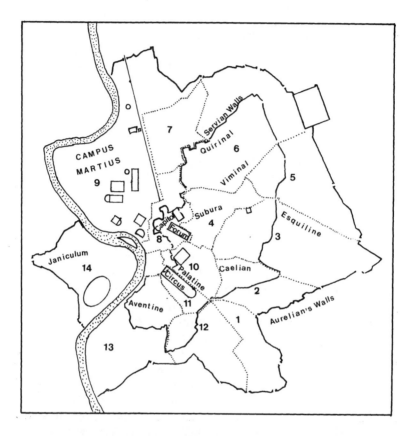

Fig. 14 Plan of Rome, as divided by Augustus into 14 regions. Note that the outer walls of the city were not built until the third century AD. Under Augustus, dense population extended to the earlier wall attributed to the King Servius Tullius; the area beyond was largely occupied by prestigious gardens.

latrines – and brothels – as the others is a reminder not to think of them as the sort of dead and depopulated archaeological parks they are now.

Augustus' concern extended down to the neighbourhood level. Whether they had any sort of formal organisation before, we cannot tell. Under Augustus each of the 265 *vici* acquired its local organisation: a group of four annually elected 'masters', *vicomagistri*, and four 'ministers', *ministri*. The masters tend to be the leading traders and craftsmen of the area, often freedmen; the ministers are mostly slaves. They proudly erected inscriptions recording their identity, depicting themselves in procession, or sacrificing to the local hearth-gods, the Lares, and to the spirit of Augustus (Fig. 15). Through this low level organisation, Augustus created a structure through which the despised tradesmen could develop a sense of self-respect and identity – and a focus of loyalty in himself.

In all these measures to contain the threat of famine, fire and riot, and to provide a network of organisation, Augustus' overriding concern was with stability. The lavishing of money on cash doles and entertainment might suggest a demagogue buying popularity. That criticism is countered by his biographer Suetonius, who is anxious to reassure us that Augustus was a responsible statesman. He cites an occasion when the mob protested about the high price of wine – to meet a severe reprimand: Agrippa's aqueducts had ensured that they need not go thirsty (ch. 42).

Fig. 15 Detail of the 'Altar of the Vicomagistri'. The ministers follow the procession carrying the statues of the Genius of Augustus in a toga (centre), and of the lares, dancing in short skirts (right).

But we should not forget that order and stability were in Augustus' personal interest: they stabilised his own regime.

Rebuilding Rome

The eyes of the world were on Rome. When Augustus put on shows, he was not simply playing to a local audience. Shows attracted vast crowds of visitors: foreign kings and ambassadors got special seating. And in general, Rome was the showplace of the empire. There will have been a large transient population, of men seeking a fortune, or justice, or just a sight of the great man.

Augustus changed the face of Rome. His famous claim to have found a Rome of brick and left it marble (Suetonius, *Augustus* 28) is a little odd in retrospect. The Roman fashion for brick-faced concrete was on the verge of starting in his reign, and the monumental Rome that impresses us now with gigantic structures like the imperial palace, the baths of Caracalla or Diocletian and the Colosseum is mostly one of brick. But Augustus' contrast was with the sun-dried brick of flimsier structures that have long since vanished. His main concern was not with vast concrete structures but with smaller-scale buildings, particularly temples and colonnaded squares. These were indeed marble, and though there had been marble buildings in Rome since the mid-second century BC (regarded then as a shocking innovation), the marble was imported, at great expense, and the supply was limited. Not until Caesar's dictatorship were the quarries at Carrara opened up, providing bright white material of an even consistency that has been the joy of sculptors ever since. The transformation must have been quite startling for contemporaries. As late as the 40s BC the Roman forum was clad in coarse limestones and peppery grey local tufas; by the end of Augustus' reign it was a forest of gleaming white marble columns, with highlights in multicoloured veneers from across the world.

Today we can only reconstruct a fragment of this programme of urban renewal – in one year alone, 82 neglected temples were repaired. Thanks to Michelangelo's redesigning of the Campidoglio, we can form little impression of what Augustus did to the Capitoline, though every visitor to Rome knows that this is the most eye-catching spot. But in two areas, that of the Forum and of the Campus Martius, we can recapture his work in some detail. The two areas offered very different challenges, and so illustrate different aspects of his aims: the Forum the historical heart of the city, full of precious relics of the past, the Campus Martius a green field site within a stone's throw of the centre, avoided for building throughout the Republic both because of its function as a parade and recreation ground and because of its physical character as a floodplain, caught in a loop of the Tiber.

The Roman Forum (Fig. 16)

There was no place so redolent of the traditions of the Roman past as the Forum. Romans were acutely aware of the link between specific places and tradition, above all religious tradition. That, according to the Augustan historian Livy, was why the Romans could never desert the site of their city: 'not a stone of her streets but is permeated with a sense of the divine' (5.51). This sense of place had been heightened by the publication of Varro's many-volumed antiquarian researches: 'we used to wander as strangers in our own city,' Cicero praised him, 'until your books effectively led us home, so that we could at last recognise who and where we were' (Cicero, *Academica* 1.9). This sense of a magical presence of the past, oozing out of each stone, and demanding hallowed reverence from the present, was not an embarrassment to Augustus. His central message was that he was leading the Romans to recover the forgotten values, traditions and rites of the past. What is fascinating about his treatment of the Forum is the way in which he could make it a museum of the past at the same time as converting it into a massive dynastic monument to his own family.

This was an area littered with potentially emotive antiques, the more effective for being battered, quaint and obscure. There was the Umbilicus Urbis, the belly-button of the city, the central pit dug by Romulus when he laid out the magical boundary of the city, and at which tradition required that annual offerings should be made. Or there was the Volcanal, or Lapis Niger, marking the spot outside the senate house where, according to one version of the story, Romulus had disappeared, whether taken up into heaven, or murdered. There were odd little shrines, to Venus Cloacina, goddess of the sewers, where Tarquin's main drains ran; or the Pool of Juturna, the nymph sister of Turnus who vainly tried to rescue him from Aeneas. These and many others we can still visit simply because Augustus chose to preserve them, not to pave them over and replace them with grander monuments. It may not sound much of a claim; but there were plenty of other areas, like the republican assembly space, with its speakers' platform and sundial, that did go under. The survivals and revivals had to be selective. So extensive was his rebuilding that rather than picturing a living tradition, we might think of his Forum as a new creation, carefully 'antiqued'.

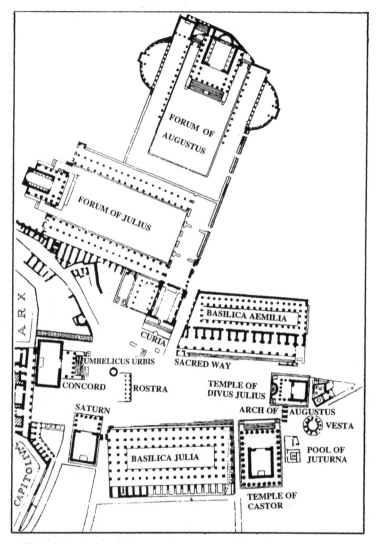

Fig. 16 The Roman Forum under Augustus (after Gatti).

He was adept at faking tradition. An inconspicuous little building in front of the senate house was the temple of Janus, two-faced god of transitions. Augustus turned it into the focus of a major ceremonial, recalling a 'forgotten' ritual of closing the brazen gates when the Roman world was at peace. He closed them three times, once more than in all past centuries put together (*Res Gestae* 13). Then there was his Parthian arch, third in a series of marble triumphal arches erected in his honour, with its elegantly inscribed lists of all the winners of triumphs and all the consuls since the foundation of the city (Fig. 17). Those lists summed up the sense in which the Forum encapsulated all preceding Roman history. And they presented Augustus as the culmination and fulfilment of tradition – the man who had won more triumphs and held more consulships than any other. But you might also say that in the culmination of tradition was its end. The last plaque finished with the last name of a Roman outside the imperial family to celebrate a triumph, Cornelius Balbus in 19 BC. There was no room on the plaque for future names, and the list was a museum piece.

The living tradition of Rome was not to do with such antiques. It had much more to do with competition. Chaotic layout and lack of overall organic planning (the Forum still looks a mess), the sense of a hubbub of competing voices from the past, of all eras, preserved in varying states of decay in buildings of all shapes and sizes, that still makes Rome a uniquely exciting place, all this Augustus came close to suppressing. The Roman name of 'monument' for any public building or construction reflects what they saw as a primary function of the building: as a reminder (*moneo* means remind) of the name and glory of the man responsible for it. But Augustus made the Forum the monument of a single man and his family.

It is perfectly true, as Suetonius remarks with surprise (ch. 29), that others, particularly triumphant generals, were allowed and even encouraged to put up their own monuments: in the Forum, Munatius Plancus, even before the embarrassment of dancing naked for Cleopatra, had renewed the temple of Saturn where the vaults of the state treasury lay, while Asinius Pollio, an independent-minded historian as well as a general, constructed a provocatively named Hall of Liberty, where records of slave manumissions were kept. There was also a cluster of 'non-imperial' monuments in the Campus Martius. But all these belong to the early period.

By the end of the reign, the monuments of the Julian family were all around. At the bottom end, away from the Capitol, the temple of Divus Julius, the divinised Caesar, dominated the central axis of the Forum, and acted as a permanent reminder of the power of the god to whom the ruling family referred its immediate origin. In front of the temple was a speaker's platform, dedicated with the bronze beaks of Antony's ships at Actium. The temple was flanked by one, or perhaps two, triumphal arches of Augustus, celebrating Actium and the Parthian 'surrender'. Then on the two sides of the Forum stretched the two largest public administrative buildings: Caesar's Basilica Julia, completely rebuilt

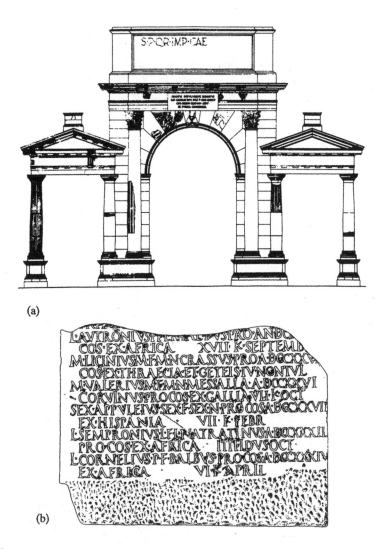

(a)

(b)

Fig. 17 (a) The Parthian arch of 18 BC, reconstructed by Gamberini Mongonet. The lists of consuls and triumphs of Rome were displayed inside the arch. Above were statues of Augustus and kneeling Parthians. (b) Fragment from the lists of triumphs, from Degrassi. The name at the bottom is L Cornelius Balbus, celebrating a triumph from Africa in the 734th year of Rome (19 BC): the marble below is chipped away to slot into a hole, and there is no further room on the lists for names.

after a fire and named after Augustus' adopted sons Gaius and Lucius Caesar; and the Basilica Aemilia, masked by a portico likewise called after Gaius and Lucius. These two, by blood remote relations of Caesar (their mother's great-grandmother was Caesar's sister), were by adoption his grandsons, so that the three generations of Caesars offered a visual continuity. The neighbouring temple of the divine twins, Castor and Pollux, eventually re-dedicated by Tiberius, had surely also been earmarked for naming by these 'divine twins', Gaius and Lucius.

The top end of the Forum was harder to reshape. But Caesar had moved around the alignment of the senate house and the Rostra, the speakers' platform of the popular assembly, to fit in with his own new complex, the Forum Julium. These Augustus remade (the senate house went up in flames at Caesar's death), and it is astonishing how he made these symbols of the Senate and People of Rome his own. The Rostra, where, grim memory, the severed heads and hands of Cicero and other enemies of Caesar had been displayed, acquired a new facade and a golden horseback statue of Augustus. The senate house, now called the Curia Julia, bore his name prominently on its facade, while inside the focus of worship, with which each session started, was the statue of Victoria commemorating his victory in the civil wars, and the Golden Shield that proclaimed his virtues (Fig. 18). The space that summed up the political history of the free Roman people had been transformed: not only had marble replaced brick and limestone, but wherever you looked in the Forum, you were confronted with the presence of Caesar's family.

(a)   (b)

Fig. 18 (a) Facade of the senate house (Curia Julia) showing dedication in the name of IMP CAESAR (i.e. Augustus). The row of columns below belong to the 'Chalcidian' portico he constructed. (b) Flying Victory with shield of virtue on a column. The shield and a statue of Victory were placed in the Curia. Sacrifice at the altar of victory was only terminated by the Christian emperors in the fourth century.

Forum of Augustus (Fig. 19)

What Augustus ended up with in the Forum was not a crude monument to his own glory, but a subtle conversion of places full of the positive feelings about the past. Augustus wanted to identify with the past itself. The glory of the good old days and the glory of the Julii were intertwined. But, like Caesar, Augustus built an additional Forum alongside the old, effectively an extension to the traditional area, but one which could be planned from new, with a much tighter architectural unity. Here his formula is the same: to identify his own glory with the past glories of Rome. If in the old Forum he and his family formed a ring of protection, so to speak, around the memory core of the Roman people, in the new Forum it was the figures of the past who formed a ring around him. The statue of Augustus, Father of his Country, stood in the centre in a chariot;

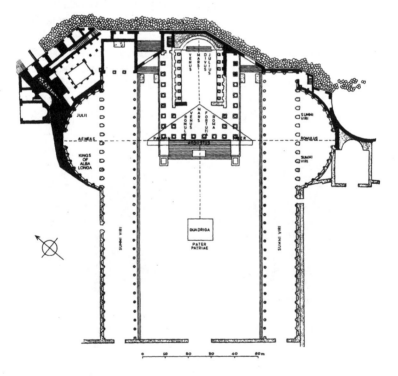

Fig. 19 Forum of Augustus, with reconstruction of sculptural programme by Zanker.

while the great Romans of the past formed two respectful files in the porticoes on either side. At the top, in two elegant semicircular areas, gathered the figures of legend: Romulus and the kings, the first founders of Rome, on one side; on the other Aeneas and his son Iulus, ancestor of the Julian clan and of the kings of Alba Longa from whom Romulus descended. As in Virgil, these ancestral figures looked down with pride towards their descendant Augustus. The temple, set at the end of this careful vista, embodied the favour of heaven towards this descendant of the gods. Mars, the cult god, had doubly vindicated Augustus, in the civil wars and in subjecting the Parthians; and he was flanked by Venus, mother of Aeneas and the Julii, and the God Julius himself. The gods and the heroes of the past all stood in silent witness to Augustus' embodiment of the virtues and values of Rome.

Another feature of this forum is worth observing. Today, the most notable standing feature is the massive curtain wall at the back (Fig. 20). It is from the traces on this wall that the elegant arcades of white columns of the forum can be reconstructed. Its technical function was to act as a fire screen: the slums of the Subura lay close behind, a common source of conflagration. But it also had the effect of isolating the forum visually.

Fig. 20 Forum of Augustus: present state. The high wall at the back is original, and indentations in the stone allow the precise reconstruction of the architecture butting up against it. The wall is over 25m high.

Like the backdrop of a theatre stage, it cut the forum off and made it a world apart, where the vision of Augustus in history was undisturbed, and where the pompous ceremonial of imperial warmaking could be celebrated. In this it was quite unlike the openness of the Roman Forum, a meeting point of many roads, accessible from all sides, and offering views in many directions. We can think of the Roman Forum as the appropriate centre of an open and outward-looking society; that of Augustus points to a closing of horizons and introspection. It was to prove the model of new fora throughout the empire. In this sense it embodies the values of a new type of society, for which the central reference point was no longer the past, but the emperor himself. For Augustus, in claiming the past as his own, had hijacked it.

Campus Martius (Fig. 21)

Outside the city boundary, in the floodplain of the Tiber, a grassy meadow where the army paraded and the young exercised, the presence of the past was less oppressive. Here was an opportunity for architects to spread their wings, away from the cramped sites and winding streets of the centre (the slightly irregular plan of the Forum of Augustus is explained by the emperor's unwillingness to force sales of property, according to Suetonius, *Augustus* 56). A traveller who knew the great cities of the eastern Mediterranean, especially the royal capitals like Alexandria of the Egyptian Ptolemies, Pergamum of the Attalids of Asia, or Antioch of the Seleucids of Syria, might express surprise at Rome's relatively homespun appearance. In this league, Rome still did not feel like the capital of a world empire. Augustus ensured, in the words of an architect of the day, that 'the majesty of the empire was expressed through the eminent dignity of Rome's buildings' (Vitruvius, *On Architecture*, preface). By the end of the reign, this area seemed to the Greek geographer Strabo one of the most beautiful in the world.

In this suburban location, Augustus allowed the names of others to stand alongside those of members of his family. The most impressive building complex here before his day was the theatre of Pompey; not just a theatre, but almost a 'leisure complex', including an enormous colonnaded square or porticus, crammed with the best collection of paintings and statues in Rome. Augustus paid for extensive repairs to the monument honouring his father Caesar's foe, magnanimously turning down the opportunity to add his own name – as he reminded people (*Res Gestae* 20). Others added to the facilities for the entertainment of the Roman people. Statilius Taurus, one of the top command at Actium, constructed

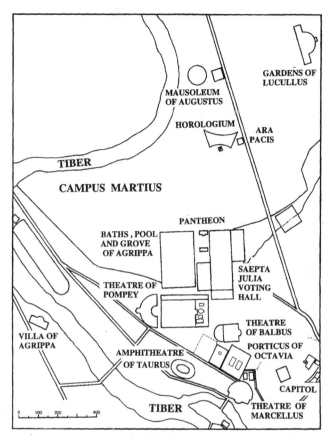

Fig. 21 Plan of the Campus Martius with new Augustan buildings.

Rome's first permanent amphitheatre in 29 BC (shows were held in open spaces like the Forum, and the Roman tradition was for the crowd to stand). Cornelius Balbus, the last man to celebrate an old-style triumph, put up another theatre, completed in 13 BC. Augustus, not to be outdone, put up a third in the same area, dedicated in the name of his nephew Marcellus: the Roman audience, once not allowed to sit, now enjoyed a wide choice of seated viewing.

Alongside the theatres, new temples and porticoes grew up. Sosius, forgiven despite commanding a wing for Antony at Actium, put up, probably in the early 20s BC, a temple of unusual sculptural delicacy to Apollo, a graceful compliment by the losing side to the power that won at Actium. Porticoes were made or restored, including one in the name of Augustus' sister Octavia. Of these buildings many fragments survive, but unlike the starkly exposed ruins of the Forum, they remain embedded in the dense medieval and later developments of this fashionable area. The most extensive development on the Campus was the work of Agrippa. Importing a fresh water supply in the Aqua Virgo, he gave Rome its first public baths – to be dwarfed by later specimens of imperial monumentalism. A park was laid out alongside, with artificial lakes and streams, walks and woods and statuary. It was here that the new voting hall stood, the Saepta Julia. Agrippa was keen to commemorate his friend Augustus, and his new temple to all the gods, the Pantheon, had a statue of Augustus in the porch, waiting to join the company inside. The Pantheon now is a very different building, and it was a handsome gesture of Hadrian to inscribe upon his masterpiece, M. AGRIPPA L.F. COS TERTIVM FECIT (Marcus Agrippa son of Lucius consul for the third time made this). It is all that remains of Agrippa's building programme.

Augustus himself was by no means an oppressive presence in all this new construction work – the reticence was deliberate. Yet one complex personally celebrated him more blatantly than any other in Rome. At the northern end of the Campus, where the via Flaminia ran close to the Tiber, stood Augustus' Mausoleum. Romans felt no qualms about building their graves before their deaths: a grand tomb was one of the best ways of advertising your name to visitors as they entered a city. Augustus' tomb was easily the largest in the Roman world (Fig. 22); yet it was already completed in 28 BC, and Augustus was to bury many of his family and friends there before his own death.

This Mausoleum, over 40 m high, and topped by a colossal bronze statue of Augustus himself, will have dominated the flat plain of the Campus Martius. It was only the beginning of a personal monument to the ruler. In 13 BC on his return from campaigns in Gaul and Germany the senate voted to put up an altar and precinct to the Peace of Augustus by the via Flaminia just south of the Mausoleum. This Ara Pacis, the loveliest surviving specimen of Augustan sculpture, was reconstructed on the 2,000th anniversary of Augustus' birth in 1937 by the fascist dictator Mussolini as a symbol of his own ambitions of world rule. But its original siting was on the side of a piazza marked out with the lines of a gigantic sundial (below, ch. 6). The pointer of this Horologium was an obelisk brought back from Egypt, recalling again the triumph of Actium. The final touch was added posthumously: it was outside the Mausoleum on two bronze pillars that he ordered to be inscribed the subtle rhetoric of his own account of his achievements, the *Res Gestae*.

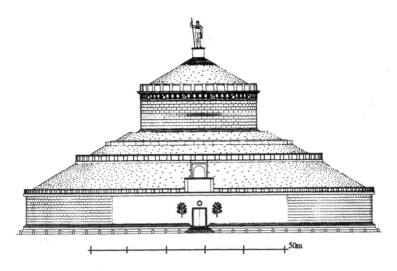

Fig. 22 Mausoleum of Augustus, reconstructed by H. von Hesberg. Laurels and oak wreath are shown around the door (cf. Fig. 8a), and a gigantic statue of Augustus on the top.

The impact of architecture

Regimes from the Pharaohs to Hitler or Ceausescu have used architecture to impress the populations under their power. Such a change of scenery can change the whole atmosphere of a society. Who was supposed to be impressed by all Augustus' building? The population of Rome itself was naturally one vital audience, and the transformation of their physical surroundings was surely as potent as the measures introduced to ensure control. But there were other, wider audiences, of the empire as a whole, and even of posterity. Naturally Augustus would be pleased to think of himself impressing us in the sophisticated twentieth century.

In embellishing Rome as befitted the 'majesty' of an imperial city, he made the city a showplace simultaneously of Rome's power in the world, and of his own power in Rome. In so doing, he transformed the function of the city. Under the Republic Rome had been the centre of power because it was the heart of the city state, where the citizens came together to compete with each other. Its monuments reflected that competition, a jumble of small-scale, individualistic buildings without overall planning. Under Augustus and his successors, Rome long remained the focus of political competition, but because it was convenient to them that it should be so. This super-city became the private monument of the emperors; and its buildings reflected not the competition among their subjects, but their own unparalleled ability to mobilise human resources. Augustus' Rome is still a Rome in transition: it begins with the restoration of the little temples, and little names, of the past; it ends with the monumental celebrations of a dynasty. The restoration of the old only provided the foundations for the new. Ovid understood, perhaps too well:

> The rude and simple style is past; now Rome is gold
> She owns a conquered world and wealth untold.
> Compare the Capitol with what it was before;
> It's a new Jupiter we now adore.
> The gleaming Palatine of Phoebus and our bosses,
> Used to be pastureland for ploughing oxes.
> Antiques may please some others; I'm relieved to be
> A modern man: this is the Age for me.
>
> (Ovid, *Art of Love* 3.113-22)

Chapter 5
Love and War

'Caesar is great.' 'But Caesar is great in war:
The tribes he conquered in the field of love are poor.'
(Propertius, Elegies 2.7.5f.)

The military dominance of Caesar Augustus lay beyond question, as he progressively drew tight his stranglehold, not just on military command, but on all the glory of war. Those who made bids for independent glory swiftly learnt their lesson. Licinius Crassus, a commander who having slain a Thracian king in combat, in 29 BC claimed the *spolia opima*, traditional award for the commander who killed his opposite number, was told that the supreme command, embodied in the power to divine the will of the gods through the 'auspices', was Caesar's. Cornelius Gallus, too boastful about his Egyptian successes, forfeited Augustus' friendship and his life. Marcus Primus, a governor of Macedonia who took his troops on a scalp-hunting expedition on his own initiative, found himself condemned in court on a charge of high treason, with Augustus volunteering himself as star prosecution witness. Victory was an imperial speciality. But did this mean that Augustus could command a total allegiance over the lives of his fellow citizens, in private as in public?

Some Romans, like Propertius, tried to set up a distinction between the worlds of war and love.

Love is the god of peace, peace lovers all adore,
It is against my mistress I wage my hardest war.
(Elegies 3.5.1)

If the love poet could define human emotions as beyond the reach of Caesar's armies, he could enjoy independence and even triumph within his own sphere. Propertius was emphatic in the distinction. When he mentions the name of Caesar or Augustus, it is almost always in the context of war: Caesar's swords, Caesar's spear, Caesar's arms, Caesar's spoils. In conceding and praising military supremacy, the love poet marks out his own sphere of privacy. The god Caesar is preparing arms against the rich Indians. The poet cheers on the troops to go and make Roman history; he looks forward to the triumph when he will applaud their progress down the Sacred Way – in the arms of his girl (3.4). The lover as soldier is an extension of this theme. If love is a military service, suitable for young men in their prime, involving guard duty at night, taking tough orders, marching across mountains and rivers, standing out at night in the cold and the rain, as Ovid puts it (*Amores* 1.9), then the two armies form alternatives. Either you serve under the standards of Caesar, or of Love. And maybe the standards of love were preferable. Whatever the Roman moralists might say about the soft effeminacy and idleness of the lover, was it not preferable to civil war? If everyone spent their lives like the lover, and lay back flat out with drink, there would be no cruel steel or warships, no Roman bones churning in the sea of Actium, no grief at the sequence of triumphs scored by Rome against herself (Propertius, *Elegies* 2.15.41ff.).

In real life the distinctions could not be so clear cut. Soldiers, after all, might themselves be lovers. What of Antony himself? His notorious love-life and heavy drinking did nothing to take the edge off his bellicosity. Plutarch says his reputation in this field went down well with the troops. In ancient imagery, the hero Hercules was a boozer and a wencher; in modern imagery, the Rambo needs his sexual fix.

These ambiguities must have come out in the sadly lost poetry of Gallus, who combined the roles of love poet and Caesarian commander in Egypt. Virgil, Propertius and Ovid treat him with respect, as the pioneer of love elegy. The few tantalising lines recovered, on a tatter of papyrus in one of the forts up the Nile where troops under his command were stationed, abruptly juxtapose the two worlds. Gallus the lover grieves at the wicked infidelity of 'his' Lycoris (his real-life lover was supposed to have been the glamorous actress Cytheris, who also kept company with Antony); but in the next line, Gallus the soldier advertises his own fidelity to Caesar, for whose day of triumph in Rome he longs. It may be Gallus who evolved the theme of love as war to reconcile the two facets of his own activity: whatever he suffered on the march, through Alpine snows or African deserts, the torments of unhappy love were worse.

Sin and war

Propertius' division of love and war turns out to be a lot more complex and difficult than at first appeared. Fundamentally different positions could be taken. Indeed, one of the most important points to grasp about the 'Augustan' poets is that they are not all saying the same thing. Virgil, Horace and Propertius were all drawn into the circle of Augustus by their friendship with Maecenas. There can be little doubt that the ruler deliberately used this cultural patronage (the poets derived large financial benefit from their association) to promote a positive image of himself in the literature of the day. But the poets do not all sing the same tune, and that alone shows that the tune was not dictated from above.

The image of Augustus of Propertius is far removed from that of Virgil, with its central emphasis on destiny and Augustus' function as an instrument of the divine plan. We see that in the *Georgics* (1.466ff.), where the young Caesar is sent from heaven to rescue Rome from an apocalypse, as well as in the *Aeneid* where he represents the long-awaited culmination and fruition of Jupiter's plans for Rome. Even further removed is the Augustus of Horace, for whom the private sphere of love acquires a central position.

For Propertius, love-making was an antidote to civil war. Horace has none of this hippy morality. Love-making was the cause of civil war. Horace is not thinking of Antony, nor of 'original sin' in the Christian sense, but of a general collapse of Roman morality. His Augustus, like that of Virgil's *Georgics*, is a saviour, sent to stop a second Flood – Deucalion, like Noah, rescued a corrupt human race from the wrath of heaven (*Odes* 1.2). But Horace is exceptionally specific about what now occasioned a second wrath of heaven. Romans were paying for ancestral sin, and would continue to do so until they had repaired the temples of the gods (*Odes* 3.6). Rome had risked destruction by the folly of civil war, and the source of that war was the pollution of the family and marriage:

> Marriage fell victim to a fault-fertile Age,
> Pollutant stain spread out from house to race,
> This fountainhead of our disgrace,
> Flooded folk and fatherland.
>
> (3.6.17-20)

There is no ambiguity about the pollution: adultery, soaked in by the Roman girl from the first lascivious dancing lessons, and put into practice with a husband's connivance at the dinner table, selling her favours to the highest bidder. That was what sapped good Italian stock, and brought a hereditary spiral of decline (21-49).

On this analysis, the termination of civil war required more than military victory. The victor must also stem the pollution, reverse the spiral of decline:

> Whoever would erase
> The godless killings, internecine folly,
> Whoever wants the praise
> Of statues to the country's father, he must dare
> Curb promiscuity.

(3.24.25-9)

It called for a deep moral reform, beyond the reach of mere legislation, a rejection of greed for gold, and the imbuing of the young with a new set of values (33-54).We cannot simply identify what Horace says with 'the official line'. We do not know whether by 23 BC, when these Odes were published, Augustus had formally proposed moral legislation, and one hopes for his sake that he did not need to commission poetic propaganda just to get his proposals passed. But at the least Horace offers an insight into one way of seeing things in Rome – one way in which the Romans could analyse their own problems, and make sense of the role of Augustus. It had nothing in common with the Propertian attempt to isolate Caesar in his war zone.

Moral reform

The moral laws enacted by the Roman assembly in 18 BC as the *leges Juliae* were part of an extensive package of legislation in Augustus' own name. Many areas of public and private life were involved, electoral bribery, luxury, public violence and probably treason. But all other laws were modifications of earlier legislation. The moral laws were quite new, though attempting to enforce a very traditional morality, and in that sense stood out as the essential item. They attempted to control extra-marital sexual relationships, and to promote marriage and procreation. It should be made clear at once that the legislation was status-specific, not a blanket affecting everyone equally, but a filter differentiating carefully between citizen and non-citizen, between slave and free, and most crucially among the free citizenry between freeborn and freed.

Roman marriage was a legal union between citizens on both sides; the offspring of a legal marriage gained citizenship and the consequent rights, particularly the right to inherit property under Roman law. Adultery was a sexual liaison outside marriage between a Roman citizen man and a married Roman citizen woman (*matrona*). The penalty was exile for both partners in crime. A husband who knowingly failed to prosecute an adulterous wife was liable to the same penalty on the grounds of living off immoral earnings (hence Horace's anxiety about women who sell themselves to Spanish traders while their husbands turn a blind eye). Other types of sexual abuse (*stuprum*) were also made illegal: between an unmarried Roman citizen woman and a man of any status, including a slave; and homosexual contact between two Roman citizen men.

But this legislation left a large and important area of extra-marital sexual activity as perfectly legal. There was nothing to stop the Roman citizen man having sex with a slave, whether male or female, whether his own property or another's. And even citizen women could be regarded as fair game if they were not 'respectable': professional prostitutes of course were excluded (it emerged as a neat way round the adultery laws for a woman to register with the aediles as a prostitute, until a scandal over senators' wives using this device under Tiberius led to the blocking of the loophole); but also those like serving girls in taverns or actresses whose job was regarded as effectively prostitution. Such disreputable professions permanently dishonoured women of any status, slave or free. But in addition there was a whole status class, that of freedwomen (*libertae*), ex-slaves who had acquired citizenship, who were exempted from the law. This is the assumption explicitly made by the Augustan poets, especially Horace and Ovid: to have an affair with a *matrona*, a *respectable* Roman lady is what Augustus forbids; the *liberta* is a legitimate object of pursuit. We do not know how the law was phrased, but the assumption of the poets is not only that there was this loophole, but that it was natural and deliberate.

One consequence of this was an exaggerated form of the sexual 'double-standard'. The freeborn Roman matron was excluded from any sexual contact outside marriage, whether with citizen or freed or foreigner or slave. Her husband, by contrast, was free to pursue any woman except a respectable freeborn citizen woman. Similarly, he could have homosexual affairs, so long as his partner was not a respectable citizen.

The distinctions, contrived and even hypocritical as they seem to us, reflect a concern for preserving the purity of the citizen body. In terms of the mechanics of the sexual act, the crucial question was not who penetrated but who *was* penetrated. A citizen might legally do as he liked with a non-citizen woman or man. What the laws guarded against was the penetration, outside marriage, of a freeborn citizen woman or man. Such penetration demeaned the dignity of citizenship, and thereby (as Horace put it) 'polluted' the citizen body.

Guarded against sexual pollution, the citizen was urged towards marriage and the production of legitimate offspring by incentives. Those married with children were given certain forms of precedence in public life, including the right to hold office at a younger age, and most tellingly, the right to inherit property from outside their own family circles. By contrast, those who between certain ages failed to marry (or even remarry) and produce children forfeited a significant part of their rights to inherit. The childless and bachelor, even after Augustus' laws, were felt to have unfair advantages in social life. The laws could do only a limited amount to redress the balance. But they enshrined a crucial new principle: that marriage and child-bearing were not purely private matters, and required the intervention of the state.

Morality and social order

We cannot satisfactorily account for the new legislation except in terms of beliefs and values that had wide, if not universal, currency within Roman society. The aim was not purely demographic, though part of the rhetoric was about the need to supply the legions with soldiers: the rise in the citizen population from just over four to just under five million in the course of the reign, registered by Augustus (*Res Gestae* 8), is better explained by the manumission of slaves and enfranchisement of provincials than by a booming birth-rate. Nor is it quite fair to suggest (as the historian Tacitus did) that its aim was to enrich the treasury with bequests illegally left to the childless, though this was an incidental effect. The basic aims emerge clearly from the debate surrounding the issue as moral.

Neither do we now, nor did the Romans at the time, have any means of scientifically demonstrating that there had been a significant 'decline' in private morality nor that it had any connection with the outbreak of civil war. What matters is how they perceived things, and what that tells us about their values. The central concern of all Romans was to achieve a stable and ordered society free from the destructive chaos of civil war. They needed to analyse for themselves what it was that made for a stable society, and what for instability. They worked by analogy. The family was an analogy for society as a whole. It was seen in ancient thought (and often is in modern) as the basic building-block of society. Cicero saw society as held together by bonds of affection, of which family ties were the first step and the model. Greek thinkers shared this analysis; but it was given an especial force in the Roman value system by their ideal of *pietas*, the relation of respect that should equally bind together members of the family, members of society, and man and god. Aeneas, by offering the archetype of Roman piety, the man who simultaneously rescues his father and son and saves, by exporting overseas, his country, reinforced the assumption that the salvation of society starts with the family.

The most persuasive way in which Augustus could account for his own conduct in civil war was by reference to *pietas*. Vengeance against the murderers of his 'father' Caesar was a good motive: his piety towards Caesar also implied piety towards Rome. The legend of the descent of the Julii from Aeneas allowed him to give especial emphasis to this line. Even without Virgil's brilliant elaboration of the myth in the *Aeneid*, the argument was already there: Caesar's heir was the new Aeneas who in saving his father saves Rome. At the same time, one of the most natural images of civil war was the analogy of the family unit: it was the war of brother against brother, 'impious' war which by the same act tore apart family and state.

In this context, it is comprehensible that the family became a focus of public debate and anxiety on a quite new scale. The morality enforced by the legislation was traditional in itself; what was new was the feeling of urgency attaching to problems of family morality. If the urgent priority was to recover a stable and ordered citizen state, was it not essential to purify the family? The significance was more symbolic than practical: by purging the impurity of sexual transgression in the citizen family, so the sin of civil war in the citizen body was washed away. For the same reason the laws remained in force, with some modifications, for over three centuries. They were felt to underpin the whole Augustan order.

Secular Games

Laws so charged with symbolic significance lent themselves to celebration, in many guises. Most immediate and conspicuous was the staging of the Secular Games in 17 BC. There was an old Roman and Etruscan tradition of marking the passing of a *saeculum*, the maximum lifespan of anyone born before the end of the last one, something over a century. Augustus transformed its significance. It was mixed up with a wholly different Greek and oriental tradition of a cycle of ages, which marked the progressive degeneration of man from a golden age of innocence, through the silver and bronze to the present age of iron. The myth offers an account of the problem of suffering: life as we know it is painful and grim not because the divine order wishes it so, but because human failure has spoiled the divine plan. But the plan remains that eventually the golden age will return. The fourth of Virgil's *Eclogues*, written in the crisis of the late 40s BC, foresaw the return of the golden age: so the Sibyl, Apollo's prophetess, had predicted.

Augustus' Secular Games drew on the emotive potential of this myth. They marked not just the passing of a generation, but of an era.

The outgoing *saeculum* was the Age of Civil War, of breakdown of state and family, a true Age of Iron. The new era was the Age of Peace, of order in the state and purity in the family. The role of Apollo received heavy stress: the god of the Golden Age, the god of purity, and of course the god of Actium, of the termination of disorder. Augustus himself played a central role: distributing the tokens of purification, he is instrumental in purging the citizen body of pollution. Horace's *Carmen Saeculare*, the official ode sung by choirs of boys and girls, is a prayer to Apollo and Diana, the chaste goddess of childbirth. The marriage laws merit an explicit mention in this prayer: Diana is asked to multiply their offspring and bring prosperity to the new decrees of the senate on marriage. But this is also a theme which implicitly holds together the Ode as a whole. The Romans, through the mouths of innocent boys and girls, are praying for fertility, human and agricultural, linked with a return of morality, of Faith, Peace, Honour and Modesty. The marriage laws more than anything else are the token of this new age of innocence.

Ara Pacis

Augustus' self-identification with the new morality went beyond authorship of the laws. Just as his victory at Actium was far more than personal, but represented the triumph of Roman values over alien debauchery, corruption and superstition, and just as his own *pietas* could be seen in the *Aeneid* to be a re-enactment of Aeneas' qualities and a model for future Romans, so his laws pointed to a way of life for which he was personally a model. When there was public protest about the harsher conditions of the law, he responded by putting his great-grandchildren on his knees. His whole family thus joined him in playing role model for the Roman happy family.

This point comes over in the Altar of Peace (*Ara Pacis*), probably the most beautiful and certainly the most symbolically charged monument of the period that survives. Put up between 13 and 9 BC on the instructions of the senate, its ostensible purpose was to welcome Augustus back to Rome after absence on campaign in Gaul. One of its most astonishing features is its complete lack of triumphal imagery. The equivalent monument in 29 BC was a triumphal arch, and if Augustus had wanted to be seen as the military figure Propertius makes of him, an arch piled with Gallic and German spoils would have been quite justified now. But the new emphasis of the *Pax Augusta* is not victory, but the quality of the paradise-like peace that his victories secure for Rome. He and his family lead the way to paradise.

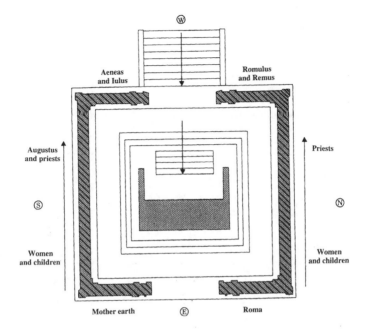

W

Aeneas
and Iulus

Romulus
and Remus

Augustus
and priests

Priests

S

N

Women
and children

Women
and children

Mother earth   E   Roma

Fig. 23 Plan of Ara Pacis, showing programme of sculptural decoration.

Fig. 24 Ara Pacis: general view from north-west (after Gatti).

Fig. 25 Ara Pacis: panel showing Aeneas, with toga drawn over head, sacrificing.

Fig. 26 Ara Pacis: detail of southern procession, showing Augustus (far left), in a pose similar to that of Aeneas, with toga over head, surrounded by priests. To the right are the *flamines*, priests of the main gods, wearing *apices*, spiked caps.

Fig. 27 Ara Pacis: panel showing mother figure with babies. Animals and vegetation indicate fertility and prosperity. The female figures to left and right appear to be both breezes and water nymphs (river water to left, sea water to right). The eighth stanza of Horace's Secular Hymn similarly enumerates land fertile with fruit and flocks, Ceres' ears of corn, healthy waters and the breezes of Jupiter.

Fig. 28 Ara Pacis: detail of southern procession. Members of Augustus' family (identifications are guesswork). The women-and-children theme echoes the mother and babies of the adjoining panel.

The structure of this unusual monument is an altar surrounded by an approximately square precinct wall (Fig. 23). The wall is broken symmetrically by doorways leading in to the altar, so that the ground-plan is of two square brackets around the altar. The marble of the monument is richly carved throughout, but the most conspicuous decoration runs round the outside of the precinct walls. The composition is elaborately balanced, visually and thematically. The doorways are each flanked by panels with mythological or allegorical scenes. The western door is flanked by Rome's mythological founders: Romulus and Remus to left, Aeneas and his son Iulus sacrificing to right (Fig. 25). The eastern door is flanked by female personifications: to the right, the goddess Roma, to the left a Madonna-like figure of the fruitful earth (Fig. 27). The north and south walls show long processions of nearly life-size figures, as if advancing solemnly from the Via Flaminia behind them to the western entrance of the altar to offer sacrifice. Beneath the processions and panels alike runs a decorative frieze of lush vegetation, curling tendrils romping with all the implausible symmetry of wallpaper design (Fig. 24).

The frieze is at one level 'historical': it preserves the memory of a particular moment, on 4 July, 13 BC, when the returning Augustus made sacrifice. But in avoiding the commemoration of any specific victory, the frieze acquires a timeless quality. It is not a record but an icon, which symbolises the values implicit in Augustus' regime. And in these values, Augustus and his family act as the vital central link. The two doorway ends contrast as male and female. The male pair, Romulus and Aeneas, may be thought of as embodying the male qualities upon which Roman success is founded: virtue and piety to the gods. The female pair represent the consequences of those qualities: the victory of Rome, and the fruitful prosperity of the earth under Rome's rule. Augustus' family, male and female, make the link between the two.

So at the head of the procession, Augustus, dressed in priestly robes and surrounded by the priests of Rome (Fig. 26), echoes the piety of his ancestor Aeneas (Fig. 25), even in the gesture by which he offers sacrifice. Behind him follow the women of his household with their children at their skirts (Fig. 28). Their ageless and classically beautiful faces frustrate the repeated attempts of scholars to do a Who's Who of the imperial family; and perhaps even for contemporaries identifications were ambiguous. What is unambiguous is the moral message. Just as the fruitful earth brings forth in abundance, in vegetation and babies (Fig. 27), so the women with Augustus are models of fertile productivity. Piety and productivity, the golden age virtues of the moral legislation, are now the most important values for which the imperial house stands; victory, the means to this end, has stepped out of the limelight.

Augustus the moral model

His role as moral exemplar gave Augustus a new significance for his subjects. It was no longer enough to do as Propertius and stand applauding at his triumphs. Now they needed – at least if they wanted a Golden Age, rather than a return to the chaos of civil wars – to absorb his values and make them their own. They must echo his piety, in revering and sacrificing to the gods of Rome, and in putting their duty to their country above their private desires. And they must do their duties as citizens in marrying and producing children. The proclamation of the Golden Age was tantamount to moral blackmail: the bachelor who preferred the pursuit of pleasure and wealth was not only breaking the law, but letting the side down for the rest of them by postponing the return to paradise.

The idea of Augustus as model can be seen at work in all sorts of ways, some quite trivial. The portraiture of the period is distinctive. The way people, at all social levels from senators to freedmen shopkeepers, liked to have themselves depicted, typically on their tombs, but also for the more distinguished in honorary statues, became distinctly reminiscent of the Leader: the same sort of poses and expressions, pious and classically serene, are found again and again, down to the same sort of haircuts (while the women imitated the classic hairstyles of the imperial ladies).

In one way all this gave Augustus a new power over his people. No longer the conqueror, or the saviour in emergency, he was the perfect Roman and the focus of their piety. But at the same time it made him more exposed. It created an enormous weight of expectation. Could he really live up to the model role he professed to set? Was his own private life so stainless? Stories about his taste for virgins were probably not too damaging – many of his successors were far more easily convicted of the fatal mixture of lechery and hypocrisy. His weak spot was his family, seen so demurely processing on the Ara Pacis. He had to exile his daughter and granddaughter for adultery, and raze his daughter's luxurious villa to the ground while he was about it. The palace, far from the model of the new morality, was a hotbed of all the intrigue, ambition, corruption and sexuality that the new age was supposed to stamp out. Awareness of that created a new tension in the relationship between ruler and ruled.

Poetry and morality

The effective intrusion of Augustus into the private and personal life of the Roman created sharp new difficulties for the poet, above all the love poet. Poetic tradition offered many models for coping satisfactorily with the figure of the military conqueror and hero. The best way was to be Homer to the conqueror's Achilles: epic was a medium in which the heroisation of warfare was natural. However, there was also a tradition, associated with Callimachus and other poets of Ptolemaic Alexandria, of preferring shorter, more elaborate and finely-worked verse to epic. But even within that tradition the conqueror could be adequately praised by subterfuge. A popular topic in the poetry of the early period of Augustus' reign is the *recusatio* – the refusal to write an epic. By emphasising what a vast undertaking it would be to write an adequate epic on Augustus, poets turned a deft compliment. No less important, they defined their own zone of personal poetry as one within which they were free to express themselves: only within epic could the conqueror reasonably demand to be the focus of attention. But the conqueror's invasion of the private sphere threw all that into question.

The tension can be felt in poetry published in the decade before the moral legislation. Propertius is explicit: his Cynthia rejoices at the removal of a law that would have forced the lovers to part, by making him marry another. He has no intention of leaving Cynthia, nor of marrying and producing children: 'there will be no soldier from my blood' (*Elegies* 2.7). We do not know whether this means there there was an actual attempt to legislate that failed, nor indeed that the real-life Propertius was a bachelor who was having an affair with a girl he could not legally marry. This is to confuse poetry with autobiography. But as a statement of the incompatibility of the pose of the love poet, free to be carried away by his own passion, with the tenor of the new morality, it could not be clearer.

Virgil too grapples with this tension. His portrayal of the relationship of Aeneas with Dido is too rich and complex to reduce to a 'message'. But what we can say is that one of the tensions it assumes is one between passion and patriotic duty. The full apparatus of contemporary Greek love poetry – the love goddess, her son Cupid, and the arrows of burning desire – are set against *pietas*. Duty prevails over passion – but without triumphalism. Aeneas and Dido are both victims, of external forces, love and duty, brought to bear upon them by the gods. Duty necessarily wins, because it has the superior force of the king of the gods and destiny behind it. But the tragedy for the human actors lies in the admission that these forces may be incompatible and tear men and women apart. That was something which the young Tiberius is said to have experienced when forced by Augustus, for reasons of state, to divorce a wife he loved, Vipsania, in order to marry one of whom he disapproved, Julia. In real life, leaving this Dido for this Lavinia did not lead to a happily-ever-after.

One solution to the tension is that adopted by Horace, to isolate the element of passion from love. He has a skill at locating his passions just over the horizon, beyond the threat of immediate danger. The names of his girls change with safe regularity, and if there are hints of feelings strong enough to hurt, they are wrapped in a nostalgic glow. Surprisingly enough, the promiscuity of the unattached bachelor fitted in better with the new Augustan morality than the quasi-monogamous loyalty of Propertius. Horace could shelter under the lovers' code propounded in his *Satires* (1.2): between the risks of classy adultery with a consul's wife, and the sordidness of resorting to the whores beneath the stinking archways, lay a happy mean of pursuit of freedwomen. The same moral duplicity that allowed the ex-slavegirl the freedom of a citizen without the protection of the adultery law allowed a bachelor poet to hymn the virtues of those very laws. Horace's flitting girls with their Greek names could be comfortably assumed, insofar as they were felt to belong to the 'real' world at all, to be freedwomen.

A similar solution lay open to Ovid, and this is ostensibly the tactic he adopts in his *Art of Love*. It may appear provocative in the aftermath of legislation bringing in severe penalties for adultery that an elegist should abandon the safe convention of writing about his own fictional love-life and instead offer a mock didactic manual on how to seduce, from the point of view of both sexes, explicitly set in contemporary Rome. But he goes out of his way to spell out that he will not trespass within the moral no-go area. In ironic allusion to the language used to warn off the profane and impure from the celebration of a holy rite, he warns the citizen women of Rome to keep away from his manual:

> I sing of sex that's safe and thefts legitimate,
> In my song nothing's criminally wrong.
>
> *(Art of Love* 1.33f.)

He anticipates with perfect accuracy that his poem may be held to incite breaking of the law – and by assertion of the conventional excuse protects himself against the accusation. The point is periodically repeated in the course of the poem. Thus in the third book, in the course of offering instructions to girls on how to pick up lovers, he offers some words on how to arrange a liaison without getting caught. But by whom? The usual elegiac scenario is getting to your lover without her *husband* noticing. But Ovid is not going to teach women to cheat on their husbands:

> The wife should fear her husband, safely under guard;
> The Law, the Leader, Shame and Right command.
> But you? Who'd guard a girl who's only just been freed?
> Come celebrate my holy mystery!

(3.613-6)

When exiled, some 10 years later, in AD 8, Ovid could offer a plausible enough defence against the charge of having 'taught obscene adultery'. In the first place, he had made clear in these passages his innocence of criminal intentions; and in the second, he was only covering well-worn topics of love poetry. Both defences are true. But it is also true that he had chosen to write in such a way as to make the *potential* conflict between love poetry and Augustan legislation as explicit as possible. He set it in contemporary Rome (he could have stuck to mythical settings). He set it in the context of contemporary legislation. Precisely by warning off the Roman matron from his work, he advertised its dangers.

You could say that Ovid was being scrupulous. But another way of looking at it is to say that he was exposing the hypocrisy of the legislation. There were two golden Romes: one the moral paradise for citizens which the new age of Augustus had brought in, where sexual modesty, *pudicitia*, reigned as in the golden age; the other the sophisticated, cultivated city, so unlike the rustic Rome of Romulus, in which the ceaseless flood of slaves ensured an ample supply of legitimate and safely 'un-Roman' sexual amusement for the Roman male. Whether or not it incites to adultery, the *Art of Love* punctures the myth of the new morality.

Chapter 6
God and Man

[An old shepherd, Tityrus, speaks]
Meliboeus, it was a god made us this peace.
To me at least he'll ever be a god, his altar
Will often soak in lamb's blood from my pens.
(Virgil, *Eclogue* 1.6-8)

Many the prayer and many the libation
Each man pours to you, and with his household gods
Includes your spirit, as does Greece in memory
Of Castor and great Hercules.
(Horace, *Odes* 4.5.33-6)

I swear by sea and earth and by the trinity,
  By your conspicuous divinity,
Greatest of men, I favoured you with backing full,
  And tried to make me yours in heart and soul.
(Ovid, *Tristia* 2.53-60)

What does it mean to call a man a god? Or rather, what did the Romans think they meant by it? From the fictional shepherds of Virgil's pastoral poems of the late 40s and early 30s BC, through Horace in hymn-like poems down to the late teens, to Ovid in his desperate attempts after AD 8 to return to favour and Rome, Roman poets treated Octavian/Augustus as someone to whom people naturally made prayers and offerings.

In trying to make sense of the attitudes behind this sort of language, we are well warned to unthink 2,000 years of Christianity. Jesus of Nazareth was born in the reign of Augustus, but the Jewish idea of a single and jealous God is a far cry from the rich polytheism of Greek and Roman pagan cults. In a sense it was much easier for a pagan to make a god out of a man. For the Greeks, there were so many grades of gods: not just the famous Olympians, but lesser spirits and local heroes. From the fourth century BC the practice grew of offering quasi-divine cult to conquerors and kings. The philosopher Euhemerus tried to explain all religion as the worship of the memory of great benefactors. The cult of the rulers of the Hellenistic kingdoms of Egypt, Syria, Asia and Macedon as 'Saviours' and 'Gods made manifest' and the like became common currency, and as the Romans in turn took over these kingdoms, their generals inherited much of this cult language.

So we can if we want play down the strangeness of Romans worshipping a human being, and say that this was no more than a convenient expression of loyalty already widespread in the eastern Mediterranean which meant little in terms of genuine religion and belief. But if we do so, we will underestimate what a revolution of attitudes the treatment of Augustus involved, and how complex and contradictory it was.

Common though ruler-cult was in the Greek east, it was controversial even there: to some an unwelcome oriental perversion, only adopted in fear and self-protection, or grotesque flattery. To Romans it might seem obnoxious, the ultimate betrayal of citizen equality and popular sovereignty. The perception that Julius Caesar was setting himself up as god and king cost him his life. And though at times the boundaries between god and man might blur, the ultimate distinction was as sharp and clear to the Roman as to us: death. Even after emperors had enjoyed various forms of cult for over a century, Vespasian underlined the distinction on his deathbed by making a joke of the fact that he was turning into a god. Only the mortal who had triumphed over death could become immortal.

Augustus' standing as man and god is as difficult a question as any theologian could hope for. The problem of what it means to say that Jesus is both fully man and fully god is at the centre of Christian theology. There is a real analogy with the problem of what it meant to call Augustus a god. His position was self-contradictory enough to permit radically different assessments. His biographer Suetonius credits him with refusing temples, except in the provinces in the joint names of himself and Rome, and says he never allowed them within the capital itself (52). Yet Tacitus voices the criticism that 'no room was left for honouring the gods, since he was willing to be worshipped with temples and cult statues by priests' (*Annals* 1.10). It does not help to deny the contradictions and smooth them over by pat formulations, along the lines of 'Augustus allowed cult of himself, but only outside Rome/only in conjunction with other gods/only of his "spirit" not of his person'.

What is quite clear is that Augustus understood the enormous political potential of manipulating religious sentiment, and that he was deft and sensitive in exploiting it. Few factors are so powerful as religion in shaping the consciousness and cohesiveness of a society. If Augustus' achievement was to reshape Roman self-awareness, to transform the perception of what 'being Roman' meant and the accepted values which held the Roman state together, a transformation of religious awareness was a vital element. He 'revived' traditional Roman religious practices and values, but in such a way as to place himself at the centre of the system. That, not whether he was really a man or a god, is the important point. The challenge was to incorporate himself into the heart of Roman religious sensibility. In order to achieve that end, he had to tread a delicate path that took him along the border between the human and the divine. We should not look for a single 'religious policy', a single catch-all definition of his position. Rather, we should observe the variety of ways in which he blurred the boundaries between the human and divine, and achieved himself an ambiguous but crucial role astride the two.

It may help to distinguish three different roles Augustus made for himself – though in reality we are dealing with a whole spectrum of positions ranging from the fully human Roman citizen to virtual identification with an omnipotent god. The first is of the man, the Roman citizen, who, far from being a god, is a model of how humans should conduct themselves towards the gods, the pious priest. The second is of the man who has claims to being regarded as a god, who deserves promotion to their company even if he is still human. The third is of the god made man; the one who is a god, but who has taken on the temporary role of humanity for the purposes of human salvation. These three should not be seen as alternative solutions, but as simultaneous. Let us look at them in turn.

Augustus as priest

There was no more reassuring way of restoring at least the appearance of Roman tradition than by 'reviving' ancestral religion. For Romans like Cicero, their traditions of auspices and augury, their priestly colleges and calendar and rites were a vital part of what Rome was about. They attributed Roman military success to religious piety – a thesis elaborated in Livy's history of Rome which surely goes back to his predecessors. The Greek Polybius too, who in the mid-second century asked himself what was the secret of Rome's success, though laying much emphasis on her constitution and military system, still regarded religion as the vital instrument by which social order was maintained. In mythological terms, the *Aeneid* shows piety as the core value transmitted by

Aeneas to the Romans; Jupiter decrees a fate of military supremacy for Rome, but it is through the piety of obedience to the will of the gods that this is achieved.

Romans analysed the collapse of the Republic as a breakdown of religious tradition, as well as of political and moral order. Old rites had been forgotten, old temples were allowed to crumble in neglect; of course the gods were angry with Rome for this gross lapse in their old piety. Whether or not there really was a 'religious decline' is quite another question. Historians have sometimes been too ready to put together the Romans' own complaints about neglect with the evidence of their use of Greek philosophy to question tradition and concluded that traditional religion had lost its meaning for them. But in that case, why were they so anxious to restore what was lost? One of the most impressive documents of Roman religious thought in the late Republic will have been the vast 15 volume study of *On Antiquities* by Varro – although it no longer survives, it formed the basis for St Augustine's refutation of paganism in the *City of God*, and is thus known at second hand. Varro's labours in digging up and preserving rites that were forgotten, or in danger of becoming so, suggest that Romans could still feel that the survival of these rites was vital for Rome. Cicero too makes clear that philosophical doubts were simply irrelevant to the value of religious tradition.

We cannot say, then, whether or not traditional religion was 'in decline' in the late Republic (there was no equivalent to figures for church attendance), but we can say that the sensation of decline and of a desperate need to reverse it opened the way for Augustus to stage a 'return' to old practices of enormous symbolic potency. Just as the rescue of moral values from the forces threatening to destroy them seemed to guarantee the rescue of the social and political order, so the rescue of endangered religious practices symbolised the preservation of order.

Above all, religious restoration guaranteed that the new order was truly Roman. Many forces seemed to threaten national identity. It was not just Cleopatra with her horrendous animal gods who threatened; there was a long history of foreign influence and dilution of ancestral ways. Greece and the Orient had been repeatedly blamed for corruption – for wealth, luxurious living and the erosion of moral standards. It was essential not only to restore order, but to signal it as Roman. Cynically, one could say that from Augustus' point of view it was handy to use emotive but politically unimportant religious rites as a smokescreen for his political revolution. But one should not underestimate the power of the genuine feelings involved: by stirring up Roman chauvinism and rejecting the corrupting influence of a foreign culture, Augustus could generate a sense of unity and identity that was precious in an unstable and diverse society.

Varro distinguished three aspects of Roman ritual, persons, place and time – who worshipped whom, where and when. In each of these areas Augustus ensured not only revival, but a conspicuous role for himself. Who held the priesthood and who held the power had been interlinked at Rome since the former dominance of patrician *gentes*. Augustus enhanced the value of the priesthood as a social marker by the multiplication of available positions, his own membership in numerous 'colleges', and by his involvement in the distribution of positions as a mark of favour. As he remarks in the *Res Gestae* (25), of the 700 and more senators who followed his standards at Actium, 83 eventually became consuls, and 170 became priests. Forgotten groups like the Arval Brethren were revived; and a vital part of their business was to offer thanksgiving on behalf of the Roman people for the welfare and prosperity of Augustus and his family. The main priesthoods were occupied by those of high social distinction; but at a lower level there were the local priesthoods of the 265 *vici* of the neighbourhoods of Rome which offered markers of local status to over a thousand of the inhabitants of the city each year.

The image of Augustus projected on the Ara Pacis (above Fig. 26), on the statue found in the via Labicana (Fig. 29), and elsewhere, is that of the priest *par excellence*. Not only is he the model of piety in general: he is the model of a specifically Roman piety, marked by the voluminous toga, drawn over his head in the proper pose for sacrifice, and equipped with the proper religious equipment (sacrificial bowls, ewers, crooks etc). The death in 12 BC of the Pontifex Maximus, his old triumviral colleague Lepidus, long since disgraced and absent from public rituals, allowed him to formalise his role as head of state religion. He was at once reviver of priesthoods, model priest, and the object of many of their prayers.

New temple building and repair of old temples transformed the setting of these rituals. Augustan restoration was of a type that would horrify the modern conservationist. If many temples were in decay, it was because the material from which they were constructed was fragile, soft tufas or even wood with terracotta decorations. The new idiom of bright Carrara marble columns with lavish Corinthian capitals imposed the characteristic hallmark of Augustus' hand even on those buildings like the temple of Capitoline Jupiter which he 'self-effacingly' re-dedicated in the name of the original builder. The mixture of modern

Fig. 29 Statue of Augustus from the via Labicana. As on the Ara Pacis, he is shown as a priest veiled for sacrifice.

materials and decorative details with old-fashioned constructional de-
signs seems not to have jarred, though for us it might suggest that
Augustan restoration was hopelessly confused with innovation.

Roman religious time was summarised in the calendar or Fasti (list
of days that were or were not *fas*, sacred). Days had their proper rituals
and festivals, and since many of these derived from the remote past, one
could say that the Fasti acted as an annual reminder of Rome's past from
its birthday (celebrated on April 21) onwards. Augustus gave the calendar a new degree of public prominence. It is now that copies of the Fasti
start to be inscribed on stone, and one of the first, at the temple of Fortune
in Praeneste, was the product of the researches of the learned Verrius
Flaccus, resident in the palace as tutor to Gaius and Lucius. Surely from
this source Ovid drew his inspiration of turning the whole calendar,
month by month, into books of elegiac verse.

It is from these calendars that we can get one of the best im-
pressions of the extent to which Augustus managed to identify himself
with Roman history and Roman religion. Quite apart from the renaming
of a month in his honour, the whole year was littered with days of
celebration for him: for his first command (Jan. 7), his 'restoration'of
the Republic (Jan. 13), his renaming as Augustus (Jan. 16), his marriage
to Livia (Jan. 17), the dedication of the Ara Pacis (Jan. 30), and so on
throughout the year with a stream of honours that broadened progressively in the course of the reign. On all these occasions thanksgivings
were offered to the gods, not just in Rome but in towns throughout Italy
and doubtless the provinces. But what matters is not just that they
celebrated Augustus, but that they did so in the context of their traditional
religion. Augustus restored tradition in order to become part of it; he
revived a religious definition of Roman identity in order to identify
himself with Rome.

Godlike man

A priest may enjoy a special closeness to the gods, but at least he stands
on the human side of the dividing line. But in a variety of ways it was
suggested that Augustus at least stood with one foot on either side of the
line. Already in the civil wars, his use of the name *Divi filius* is indicative.
His posthumous 'adoption' in Caesar's will enabled him to adopt the
name form, Gaius Julius Gaii filius Caesar (Octavianus). The deification
of Caesar as Divus Julius was the basis for the substitution of an
unparalleled patronymic; and he emphasised the point by dropping Julius
from the name – not merely son of the divine Julius, but Son of the

Divine, or Son of God. Combined with the honorific first name of Imperator (awarded by the senate in 39), it produced the portentous style Imperator Caesar Divi filius in which no element of standard Roman nomenclature remains. After 27 BC, the finishing touch was put to his title, Imperator Caesar Divi filius Augustus. The conventions of Roman name style had become a vehicle for mystification. Gaius and Lucius likewise were described as Divi nepotes, grandsons of god, and with the same implication, that the descendants of a god should in turn inherit his divinity. Of course, Augustus' own consecration as a Divus took place immediately after his death.

Suetonius' biography of Augustus is firmly that of a mortal: even posthumous deification did not make Romans think he was a god except in a special sense. Yet there are elements of myth-making that belong to another sphere. At the end of the Life (ch. 94) he offers a cluster of 'signs' that indicated a more than human nature. They include some striking points of similarity to the gospel narratives of the birth of Christ. The senate is supposed, with ludicrous implausibility, to have decreed a ban on rearing male Roman babies in the year of Augustus' birth because of a portent indicating that a king of Rome had been born. On top of this 'slaughter of the innocents', we are offered an Annunciation: his mother Atia dreamed during a visit to the temple of Apollo that the god had visited his favour on her in the form of a snake; Augustus was born nine months later (similar tales were told of the birth of Alexander the Great). The difficulty with stories like this is to know what currency they had and when. Did Augustus deliberately put about the tale that he was the natural son of Apollo, or did hagiographers invent it after his death? Either way, such myths are part of the attempt to bridge the gulf between man and god.

A convenient idiom for linking man and god is assimilation: the god can be represented with the features of the man, or the man with the attributes of the god. Augustus is 'assimilated' in this way to a wide range of gods. One beautiful example is an agate ring stone cut in the late thirties on which Octavian is shown as the god Neptune, riding in a chariot across the waves – and over the head of his unfortunate foe (Fig. 30). The features are those of Octavian; the naked body and the trident and the sea-chariot point to Neptune. The image evokes not only naval victory, but symbolically the bringing of calm after a storm. This is the picture of the sea god as bringer of calm depicted by Homer, and the political analogy is underlined by Virgil in a memorable passage at the beginning of the Aeneid where Neptune calms the storm troubling Aeneas' fleet: it is like the situation in a riot when the people catch sight

Fig. 30 Agate ring stone. Octavian in the guise of Neptune (note trident) rides over the waves. The head of an opponent, probably Sextus Pompey rather than Antony, is seen under the sea-horses' hooves.

of a man of great piety and achievements, and a silence falls on them (1.145-56). Octavian is like Neptune because he calms the waters of civil war.

A ring stone is a private commission. A more explicit official status can be allowed to the images propagated by the coinage of the state. There is no surprise that the head of Augustus becomes the normal 'head' on most Roman coinage, including much local coinage around the empire, so displacing the traditional heads of deities, like the goddess Roma of early Roman coinage. But though here the authority of Augustus stands in the place of divine authority, it is not the same as an assertion of immortality. We come much closer to an identification with the divine in the beautiful and imaginative series of silver coins struck around the time of Actium (possibly to finance the war). The theme of the series is the link between Imperator Caesar and the gods. On one side we see a deity: Venus, Victory, Peace, Jupiter or Apollo; on the other Caesar with some of the symbols of the respective god. God and Caesar swap places between each other on heads and tails: either the god provides the larger head and Caesar a smaller figure on the reverse, or vice versa. One might say that this suggested no more than Virgil's image of Augustus going into battle at Actium supported by the gods; yet it is

Fig. 31 Two denarii of Octavian, around the time of Actium. (a) To the left, Octavian is shown on the head (top), a herm of Jupiter on the tail.(bottom). (b) To the right, the head of the herm of Jupiter on the head has the features of Octavian (top); on the tail (bottom), Octavian sits on a consul's throne holding a statue of victory.

notable how his features are assimilated to those of the gods. One pair in particular shows Caesar twinned with a 'herm' (statue in the form of a head on a pillar) of Jupiter in his guise as the thunder god, marked by a thunderbolt. But the features of the god are unmistakably those of Caesar (Fig. 31).

Later coinage may avoid such blatant identification, though an *element* of the superhuman underlies every imperial image. But its advantage is to reveal the close tie between the language of official image-making ('iconography') and the language of the poets. When Horace in *Odes* 1.2 searches among the gods for a possible saviour, and turns in prayer to Apollo, Venus, Mars and finally Mercury, 'the winged son of Maia, you imitate in transfigured form a young man and let yourself be called Caesar's avenger' (41-4), this does not mean that there was a cult of Mercury/Augustus; but it does reflect the same attempt to make sense of Augustus by assimilation.

One approach much favoured by the poets is to establish a parallelism of function, especially between Jupiter and Augustus:

> Thundering Jupiter we did believe of old
> The king of heaven; a present god on earth
> Will be Augustus as his conquests add
> Britain and Persia to the imperial fold.
>
> (Horace, *Odes* 3.5.1-4)

If we read the pair of coin types in this light, there is no assertion that Augustus and Jupiter are identical, but rather that Augustus performs a function on earth parallel to that of Jupiter in heaven.

This idea lies behind Ovid's comparison of the Palatine to the home of the gods at the end of the Milky Way, and many other passages. On the Gemma Augustea also (Fig. 11) Augustus has the sceptre and eagle of Jupiter. The divine order in heaven and the human order on earth are seen as parallel systems. Order on earth, secured by Roman imperialism, is a reflection of the greater celestial order. As Jupiter, king of the gods, is the source of the supreme cosmological order, a Jupiter-on-earth is needed to transmit this order to chaotic humanity. Augustus, human by definition, performs this divine role.

We should beware of regarding this sort of language, so common in the poets, as merely a form of flattery to keep Augustus sweet, a type of over-the-top hyperbole permitted by poetic licence but inappropriate in the prose of real politics. Better to take it as a genuine attempt to make sense of Augustus' extraordinary position. His role could not be adequately described and accounted for in traditional terms, in the language of the Roman *res publica*. It was necessary to reach outside the Roman state to a higher level of justification. Casting Augustus as a Jupiter-on-earth gives him the necessary ambivalence: at once an insider, a good Roman citizen, and an outsider, bringing to Rome not the humiliation of a foreign order (Hellenistic kingship) but a closer approximation to the divine order which pious Romans acknowledged.

The Saviour

After two millennia of Christianity, the assumption has become embedded in our culture that the worlds of politics and of religion *ought* to be kept apart. We find any suggestion of a politician being treated as a god absurd; never more so than when the language used of him appears to have specifically Christian overtones. Historians have been loath to admit that the language used of Augustus might actually be in some ways parallel to that used of Christ. Yet the suggestion is neither absurd nor even blasphemous, for the attempt of Christians to define a historical man as a god was made in a political and religious context transformed by Augustus. The gulf between the two thought-worlds is immense; yet the links are enough to show that attempts to categorise the divinisation of Augustus as 'purely political' must be suspect.

In the Christian tradition, there is room for a figure who mediates directly between heaven and earth: who when human order breaks down brings a human embodiment or 'incarnation' of the divine order down to earth as a model around which human society can redirect itself. The classic vision of this 'Saviour', which the Christian tradition sees fulfilled in the person of Christ, is that of the Jewish prophet Isaiah:

> The people who walked in darkness have seen a great light.... For a boy has been born for us, a son given to us to bear the symbol of dominion on his shoulder; and he shall be called in purpose wonderful, in battle God-like, Father for all time, Prince of peace.
>
> (Isaiah 9.2 and 6)

The promised one is seen as both a great conqueror and a source of wisdom, justice and godliness; and the peace he brings to human society is mirrored by a peace within nature:

> Then the wolf shall live with the sheep and the leopard lie down with the kid; the calf and the young lion shall grow up together, and a little child shall lead them...the infant shall play over the hole of the cobra, and the young child dance over the viper's nest.
>
> (Isaiah 11.6-9, New English Bible)

Paradoxically, despite the deep gulf between the monotheistic Jewish tradition and Roman polytheism, it is precisely at this key point for the development of Christianity that allowed a compromise of strict monotheism by the insertion of a god-made-man, that the two traditions converge. For in representing Augustus as a god-made-man, the Romans were not simply adding Augustus *alongside* their other gods, but placing him as a new *intervening* layer between gods and men.

Human peace and prosperity could no longer be achieved by direct appeal from man to god; the overall structure of peace was *dependent* on the god-made-man. Piety to the gods was no longer enough: a precondition of the gods' support was now piety to Augustus.

We can observe something of the process by which the idea of the Saviour was developed at Rome. The pastoral poems of Virgil include one, dated to 40 BC, in the form of a prophecy of the return of the Golden Age (the 'Messianic' Eclogue, 4). The prophecy is attributed to the Sibyl of Cumae, under the inspiration of Apollo. The agent of the return to the golden age is a newly born 'wonder child': he will free man of the remaining traces of sin, and pacify and rule the world. At his birth a more than pastoral state of nature at peace will ensue:

> The goats will come home by themselves with milk-filled
> udders,
> Nor will the cattle be in fear of great lions...
> The serpent will perish, and the treacherous herb of poison
> Will perish...
> *(Eclogues* 4.21-5)

The apparent link between Isaiah and Virgil is possibly no coincidence, for Jewish ideas were indeed transmitted to the west in a variety of forms, including that of 'Sibylline oracles' in Greek hexameters. Surviving examples of such oracles, a strange amalgam of Greek and Jewish ideas dating over several centuries, include this sort of Messianic prophecy:

> Rejoice, maiden, and be glad, for to you the one
> who created heaven and earth has given the joy of the age.
> He will dwell in you. You will have immortal light.
> Wolves and lambs will eat grass together in the mountains.
> Leopards will feed together with the kids...
> Serpents and asps will sleep with babies
> and will not harm them, for the hand of God will be upon
> them.
> *(Sibylline Oracles* Book 3, 785-95)

Of course, we cannot be sure that precisely this sort of material was available to either Virgil or Augustus. But Sibylline prophecies of some sort were certainly a concern to Augustus, who was well prepared to exploit such material, however alien. Among his measures to impose order was to gather together all supposed Sibylline prophecies, and through the priestly college that traditionally had responsibility for such prophecies (the Board of 15) to burn the 'false' prophecies, and store the 'genuine' safely – in the new temple of Apollo on the Palatine. A Sibylline prophecy of the new *saeculum* was officially invoked for the Secular Games, organised by the same Board of 15, and Horace's Ode makes clear that it was a prophecy of a Golden Age, with a return of justice. Whether or not Virgil's prophetic Eclogue was allowed official status, it reflects 'Sibylline' prophecies that were officially endorsed.

Virgil takes up his earlier theme again in the *Aeneid* in the scene of Aeneas' descent to the underworld. First, by setting this descent at Cumae, with the Sibyl as guide, he brings the episode into explicit contact with the Sibylline prophecies of Roman state religion. Aeneas' promise of a marble temple to Apollo and a home for the Sibyl's prophecies (6.69-74) further underlines the link with the new Palatine temple ('marble' leaves no doubt about the date of construction). When the Sibyl sees Augustus in the underworld, she then alludes explicitly to her own prophecies, whether in Virgil's earlier poem, or the 'official' prophecies that lie behind it:

> This is the man, this is he, whom you have often heard
>   promised:
> Augustus Caesar, descendant of a god, who will again
>   establish
> The golden ages which once reigned in the fields of Latium
> Under Saturn of old, and who will carry forward empire
> Over the Garamantes and Indians...
>
> (6.791-5)

The *Aeneid* is a poem, not an official document, though it carried an almost biblical authority as a statement of Roman values. We cannot infer from it that Augustus expected formal acknowledgement as a Saviour figure, and indeed in the proceedings of the Secular games, which were publicly inscribed in some detail, his role is of the pious priest, not of the promised one of the Golden Age. Nevertheless, this sort of idea was in circulation, and as such exploited by him.

Two examples of Augustan exploitation of quasi-messianism may be looked at briefly. One is a decree of the assembly of the province of Asia, inscribed and disseminated in several copies, dating probably to 9 BC. The assembly had offered an award for the best honour proposed to Augustus, and the winner was the proconsul of the province, Paulus Fabius Maximus. The honour, simple enough in itself, was to make

Augustus' birthday, 23 September in the Roman calendar, New Year's day in the local Greek calendar. What is remarkable is the evangelical fervour of the language in which this step was expounded and justified:

> ...the most divine Caesar's birthday, which we might justly consider equal to the beginning of all things.
> ...He has given a different appearance to the whole world, which would happily have gone to utter ruin, had not Caesar been born to the common good fortune of mankind. Therefore each of us would justly reckon [his birthday] to be the beginning of his own life, since that day was the end of regretting that we had been born.

By making the birth of Augustus, rather than the political turning-point of Actium, the beginning of the new age, he is given a role going well beyond that of conqueror and statesman. The assembly welcomes the proposal as 'good tidings' (*euangelia*) – 'the beginning of good tidings for the world was the birthday of the god' – and thanks Providence for the benefit to mankind in sending him, 'as a saviour for us and our descendants, to bring war to an end and set all things in order'. Such exotic language may have been more at home in the Hellenistic east than at Rome; yet the author of the decree is a Roman proconsul and a member of the old Roman aristocracy.

For a second example, we may turn back to the sundial on the Campus Martius, near which we have seen Augustus' Mausoleum and the Altar of Peace stood (Fig. 32). The theoretical reconstruction of this sundial, and its confirmation in the excavation of a fragment, is one of the most dramatic contributions of archaeology to our understanding of Augustus. The layout of such a sundial required mathematical and astronomical calculations of enormous sophistication. It was at this time, and surely by the same mathematicians, that the original calculations by which Julius Caesar had established the year as a regular 365 days adjusted by the occasional leap year were finally corrected so that the leap year should fall, as it has ever since, every fourth, rather than every third, year. These reforms of the calendar earned their implementers the new month names of July and August. The whole idea of a sundial which could accurately indicate both hour and day of the year depended on the establishment of a mathematically reliable calendar.

But for the Romans astronomical calculations carried a further vital symbolic dimension. The complex but beautiful predictability of the movements of heavenly bodies seemed, to the ancient mind, to

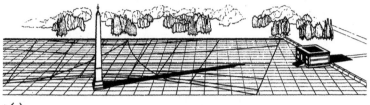

(a)

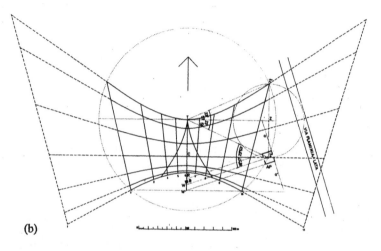

(b)

Fig. 32 Reconstruction of the Solarium of Augustus by Buchner. (a) View of obelisk as pointer of sundial, throwing shadow on central line on Augustus' birthday, towards the Ara Pacis; (b) mathematical calculations of the network of the sundial, including the positioning of the Ara Pacis.

embody the ability of the divine world order to impose a beautiful and regular order amidst seeming chaos. The chaos of human life might make sense if it were governed by mathematical rules as regular as those of astronomy. Astrology is thus an attempt to make sense of the apparent rulelessness of our life by the imposition by analogy of the complex predictability of the heavens. If our lives are governed by the infinite permutations of the conjunctions of heavenly bodies, then there is a divine order on earth too.

Such thought was popular and powerful at this period – understandably so when the acute unpredictabilities of a period of civil disorder gave urgency to attempts to discover order at symbolic levels. On more than one occasion Augustus expelled astrologers from Rome: their predictions of change in the political order could be a source of political instability. But his best weapon was to represent his own order as astrologically preordained. Among the signs reported by Suetonius (ch. 94) was the result of his visit to the astrologer Theogenes in Apollonia (i.e. at the time of Caesar's death). Such was his horoscope that Theogenes fell to his knees and adored him, and, continues Suetonius, such was Augustus' subsequent confidence in his own horoscope that he published it and struck coins with the sign of Capricorn. Why Capricorn should be the sign for one born on September 23, the sources do not explain. It is reasonable to guess that it pointed to the moment of his conception nine months before, on December 23, a day on which his mother dreamed she had been visited by Apollo.

The sign of Capricorn is indeed widely found, not only on his coinage, but in other contexts like the Gemma Augustea (above, Fig. 11). The details of representation spell out the message (Fig. 33): the cornucopia on its back points to prosperity, the rudder beneath to ordered government, and the globe between its hooves to rule over the world. Augustus, that is to say, was preordained by the gods to rule the earth, bringing peace and prosperity. Because his birthday fell on the equinox, half way, that is, between the sun's highest point on midsummer day, and its lowest on midwinter day, his 'birthday line' bisected the square. Only on the equinox did the shadow cast by the tip of the pointer, a great Egyptian obelisk, traverse the square in a straight line; on other days it followed a curve (Fig. 32a). This line passed through the centre of the

Fig. 33 Coin of Augustus, showing astral sign of Capricorn, with cornucopia, rudder and globe. The Capricorn appears on many issues from 27 BC onwards.

Altar of Peace, which also lay at the crossing point with a circle centred on the midwinter or Capricorn point (Fig. 32b). The mathematical details are (by definition) highly complex and obscure, but what must have been obvious to the simplest Roman was an association of ideas: Augustus' birth, Augustus' conquest (the obelisk, naming Egypt), and the peace, prosperity, piety and purity of his regime (depicted on the altar). All these things could be seen to be inscribed in the stars and the passage of the sun, in a divine plan interwoven in the structure of the universe. The sundial was an alternative expression of the Saviour role described by the Asian decree or the *Aeneid*, of the man born to bring back paradise.

The majesty of Augustus

Through the three simultaneous roles of the man of supreme piety to the gods, the man taking on the role of the gods, and the instrument of divine fate, Augustus occupied an ambiguous but spectacular status as the intermediary between earth and heaven. The details of the various forms of cult or quasi-cult offered to him in provinces, towns and street-corners throughout the world are beyond the scope of this book. Together they formed a vital focus of loyalty and force for cohesion across the empire. We need not assert that worshippers 'believed' Augustus to be a god like other gods, let alone that he made traditional worship superfluous. But there is no reason to deny that his cult was genuine and serious. It offered an important way of making sense of the world, and of coming to terms with the 'divinely ordained' position of Roman rule and Augustan dominance.

But that does not mean that everyone was now in fact united in adoring loyalty to the new leader. Paradise did not return, and the Romans did not live happily ever after. On the contrary, Augustus' solutions in themselves created new problems. Naturally Augustus had enemies, including those who for whatever reasons were prepared to risk an assassination attempt; of course these did not think him divine. But more important, we should recognise that the very language that elevated him as divine could in itself be used as a weapon in human conflict. It became normal, because of the quasi-divine authority of the name Augustus, to invoke him in oaths. His images were treated with exceptional respect as inviolable: that was one good reason for cities throughout the empire putting his head on their coins; and the convention rapidly grew up of treating his statues as a place like a divine altar where slaves fleeing the wrath of their masters could take refuge. To break an oath by Augustus, to deface his image, to violate the sanctuary of his statue was to show disrespect to his greatness, his *maiestas*. And though the emperor himself might have no interest in such trivia, at grass-roots level the attractions of such an accusation were enormous. If you could show that your rival was guilty of abusing Augustus, you showed that he was an enemy of the whole order which depended on Augustus. Disrespect to the divine *maiestas* was the ultimate treachery. The charge was rapidly assimilated to the existing legislation against contempt for the majesty of the Roman people.

Augustus had a laudable reputation for ignoring such accusations, and his successor Tiberius endured the odium of responsibility for a charge which did more than anything else over the next reigns to embitter relations between emperors and senate. But the roots of the problem lie in the Augustan myth. The more that the peace, order and stability of the Roman world were identified with Augustus' person, the harder it became to tolerate any even apparent expression of disloyalty to his person. The inevitable victim was that fundamental Roman value, freedom of self-expression, *libertas*.

A value system which creates unity out of intense loyalty to a central focus, must in its nature be intolerant of divergent values. Augustus' reign ends with clear indications of such fundamentalist intolerance: the burning of the histories of one Titus Labienus, who was imprudent enough to take a 'republican' stance; the exile of the orator Cassius Severus for speaking disrespectfully of leading men; and the banishment of Ovid to cold Tomi for writing incautiously about love.

Augustus tried to bind together a fragile Roman world not only by military force but by common values, values derived from Roman tradition and consciously stamped with Romanness. He placed himself at the centre of that value system. His legacy was three centuries of fluctuation between order and disorder. But the values in many respects endured, until the final major transformation by Constantine, which put Christ alongside the emperor at the heart of the system.

Augustan Authors (Who's Who)

Some basics about authors writing during, or about, Augustus' reign.

Augustus The emperor left behind various records of his own life. His Autobiography has not survived. Instead we have the record of achievements, *Res Gestae Divi Augusti*, which he left on his death to be inscribed outside his Mausoleum. Copies were inscribed round the empire, and the text we have comes mainly from Ancyra (modern Ankara). It details offices and honours held, benefactions to the Roman people, and victories won.

Cassius Dio Greek historian writing in early third century AD. In his many volumed history of Rome down to his own times, books 50-6 cover the Augustan period, and are important as the only surviving detailed chronological narrative.

Cicero Rome's greatest orator, born 106 BC, in the final year of his life threw his support behind Octavian against Antony in the *Philippics*. Whether his political thought (especially in the *Republic*) influenced Octavian is an open question. Certainly Octavian learnt much from his techniques of persuasion. Victim of the triumviral proscriptions of 43 BC.

Horace Born 65 BC, held rank under Brutus at Philippi. Recruited through Maecenas to support of Augustus. Though claiming to avoid political themes, repeatedly praises Augustus. A fragmentary *Life* by Suetonius quotes friendly correspondence with Augustus. Published *Satires* I c. 35, *Satires* II and *Epodes* c. 30, *Odes* I-III c. 23, *Epistles* I c. 20, *Carmen Saeculare* for performance at Secular Games of 17, *Epistles* II and *Ars Poetica* c. 20-13, *Odes* IV c. 13. Died 8 BC.

Livy Born 59 BC, wrote history of Rome from foundation to 9 BC in 142 books. Surviving books cover the earliest period (i-x), the Punic Wars and the early second century BC (xxi-xlv). Though only summaries survive of his account of Augustus, there are allusions from the first book onwards to contemporary Rome after 28 BC.

Maecenas Close friend of Octavian in the civil wars, avoided senatorial status and overt political involvement, but acted as representative and agent. An amateur poet, he cultivated the friendship of a group of poets, Horace, Propertius, Varius and Virgil, in the 30s and 20s, who dedicated several poems to him. Possibly compromised by links through his wife to a conspirator in 22 BC, seems to fade from the scene before his death in 8 BC.

Ovid Born in 43 BC, educated in Rome, successful rhetorical performer, opted against senatorial career. His *Amores* and *Heroides* (first published after 16 BC) proved the culmination of the Roman tradition of love elegy. The *Ars Amatoria* of c. 1 BC, in teaching seduction, came provocatively close to conduct forbidden by Augustus' laws; this was one ground for his exile to Tomi in AD 8. The epic *Metamorphoses*, and the poetic calendar, *Fasti*, were composed (if not completed) before the exile. The *Tristia* and *Epistulae ex Ponto* argued his case for defence – or mercy.

Plutarch Greek philosopher, essayist and biographer, writing late first/early second century AD. His parallel *Lives of Greeks and Romans* include a fine Life of Antony, used by Shakespeare.

Propertius First major Roman elegiac poet, from Assisi, fought Octavian in Perusine War (41-0 BC). The first three books of his *Elegies*, published through the 20s, revolve round amatory themes, and include dedications to Maecenas; the fourth (c. 16 BC) turns to Roman myths. In this as in his early books he professes to imitate the Alexandrian poet Callimachus.

Suetonius Man of learning and biographer, early second century AD, writes *Lives of Caesars* from Julius to Domitian, also lives of famous authors including Augustan poets. The Life of Augustus is exceptionally well-researched, drawing on a wide range of sources and documents including private correspondence.

Tacitus The greatest historian of the early empire, writing early second century AD. The *Annals* begin with the death of Augustus and accession of Tiberius, but contain a number of illuminating back references to Augustus, notably the memorable sketch in the first ten chapters of Book I.

us Roman love elegist contemporary with Propertius. His patron was Messalla, not Maecenas; he avoids overtly political themes.

Velleius Author of a summary history of Rome down to Tiberius, under whom he held military rank, published AD 30. Strongly panegyrical in approach to Tiberius, he is valuable for offering one possible 'loyalist' line on key incidents of Augustus' reign.

Virgil Born c. 70 BC near Mantua; family lost land in Octavian's distributions. His poetry is marked by subtle but powerful engagement with contemporary affairs; the support of Maecenas played a significant role. The ten pastoral *Eclogues* (42-39 BC) draw on contemporary disruptions of the countryside; the didactic *Georgics* (29 BC) teach farming in the context of the close of civil wars; the epic *Aeneid* uses the myth of Augustus' 'ancestor' Aeneas to redefine Rome's greatness. Died 19 BC.

Vitruvius Dedicated to Augustus, whom he served as military engineer, his ten books *On Architecture* (early 20s BC?).

Suggestions For Further Study

One way to move on from this book to further study is to look *critically* at the themes it raises by going back to the sources and asking whether your reading agrees with mine, and what else can be said. Examples in each chapter would be as follows.

1. *Actium.* Read one or more of the poetic accounts of the battle in Virgil (*Aeneid* 8.675-728), Horace (*Odes* 1.37) and Propertius (*Elegies* 4.6) (also perhaps the prose accounts in Dio 50.12ff. and Plutarch, *Antony* 62ff.). What is (and is not) being said about the battle? What do the different pictures do for the image of Augustus? Do you detect undercurrents of irony in any of them?

2. *Metamorphosis.* Look at some different accounts of the Augustan political settlement: Augustus' own in the *Res Gestae* (esp. 1-7 and 33-4); Dio's account of 27 BC (Book 53.2-18); Suetonius' positive analysis of his reign (*Augustus* 28-60); and Tacitus' devastating exposé of the basis of his power in *Annals* 1.1-4 and 9-10. Does Augustus' behaviour come across to you as a cynical pursuit of personal power or a statesmanlike reform for the benefit of Rome? Did he set out to persuade or to deceive? Did he sacrifice the liberty of the citizen to the security of his regime?

3. *Palace and court.* Among the best insights into the Augustan imperial family are Suetonius' biographical accounts of the early lives of family members who later became emperors, notably Tiberius (chs 4-22) and Claudius (chs 1-4); see also Augustus 62-73 on his family and private life. Is it just sensationalism ('tabloid journalism') to enquire in this way into what went on behind palace walls, or were there serious political issues at stake?

4. *Golden Rome.* Take an Augustan monument, like the Forum of Augustus or the Ara Pacis or just the Gemma Augustea (it will help to have pictures from other publications in addition to this). Try to imagine

what impact it would have on the ancient viewer; how and in what context the Roman visitor would experience it; how they would work out any 'messages' in it; what it would say to them about Augustus and his power. How effective do you think this sort of manipulation of opinion would be?

5. *Love and war.* Read some Augustan love poetry, e.g. some of Propertius, *Elegies* I, Horace, *Odes* I, Ovid, *Art of Love* I. Do Horace and Propertius keep the themes of love and politics separate? Where, and with what effect, do they overlap? Is Ovid playing the same game? Can anything in Ovid (or the others) be taken as deliberate provocation or questioning of Augustan morality?

6. *God and man.* Read some of the poetic passages that make a god out of a man: Virgil, *Eclogue* 4 with *Aeneid* 6.791ff. and *Georgics* 1.463ff.; Horace, *Odes* 1.2, 1.12 and 4.5. What boundaries do the poets make between gods and men? How do they take Augustus across those boundaries?

Suggestions For Further Reading

Politics and society

A constant challenge in approaching Augustus is the need to understand something of Rome before he transformed it. Approachable introductions are M. Beard and M. Crawford, *Rome in the Late Republic* (London, 1985) and T.P. Wiseman (ed.), *Roman Political Life 90 BC-AD 69* (Exeter, 1985). P.A. Brunt, *The Fall of the Roman Republic* (Oxford, 1989) is the vital scholarly work on the theme. On Octavian's rise to power, J.M. Carter, *The Battle of Actium* (London, 1970). On the myths generated around the figure of Cleopatra, there are interesting studies by Lucy Hughes-Hallett, *Cleopatra: Histories, Dreams, and Distortions* (London, 1990) and Mary Hamer, *Signs of Cleopatra* (London, 1993). On Augustus' reign, D.C.A. Shotter, *Augustus Caesar* (London, 1991) offers a succinct introduction to the main political themes. A.H.M. Jones, *Augustus* (London, 1970) remains valuable for its thematic approach. The forthcoming chapters by J.A. Crook on Augustus in the new edition of the *Cambridge Ancient History* vol. X are admirably lucid and balanced. The classic political narrative remains R. Syme, *The Roman Revolution* (Oxford, 1939): its roots in the politics of the 1930s and its lapidary style have given it lasting value. The collection of essays in honour of Syme, *Caesar Augustus: Seven Aspects*, edited by F. Millar and E. Segal (Oxford, 1984) has excellent contributions on many vital themes. There are useful essays too in *Between Republic and Empire: Interpretations of Augustus and his Principate*, edited by K.A. Raaflaub and M. Toher (Oxford, 1990).

Art and archaeology

Some of the most important recent contributions to the understanding of the period have come from archaeology. Outstanding is Paul Zanker, *The Power of Images in the Age of Augustus* (translated by Alan Shapiro, Michigan, 1988). Some of the most important discoveries are still inaccessible in English: Augustus' house on the Palatine (inadequately published in German by G. Carettoni, *Das Haus von Augustus* [Mainz, 1984]), and the dramatic sundial of the Campus Martius (E. Buchner, *Die Sonnenuhr des Augustus* [Mainz, 1982]). There is much of relevance in the survey article by John Patterson, 'The city of Rome: from Republic to Empire' *Journal of Roman Studies* 82 (1992) 186-215. On Augustus' monument at Actium, see W.M. Murray and P.M. Petsas, *Octavian's Campsite Memorial for the Actium War* (Philadelphia, 1989).

Literature and politics

The bibliography on the poets is too extensive to survey. Full details on individual poets are available in the *Cambridge History of Classical Literature* vol. 2, part 3, *The Age of Augustus*, edited by E.J. Kenney and W.V. Clausen (Cambridge, 1982). For a general essay, see J. Griffin, 'Augustus and the poets: "Caesar qui cogere posset" ', in *Caesar Augustus* (above) pp. 189-218. Recent contributions to the theme of poetry and politics include A.J. Woodman and D.A. West (eds), *Poetry and Politics in the Age of Augustus* (Cambridge, 1984); J. Griffin, *Latin Poets and Roman Life* (London, 1985); H.-P. Stahl, *Propertius: 'Love' and 'War'. Individual and State under Augustus* (Berkeley, 1985); P.R. Hardie, *Virgil's Aeneid. Cosmos and Imperium* (Oxford, 1986); D. Kennedy, *The Arts of Love* (Cambridge, 1992); Anton Powell (ed.), *Roman Poetry and Propaganda in the Age of Augustus* (Bristol, 1992).

Source material

To make Augustan Rome come alive, you must go back to contemporary material. A wide range of material is collected for the Open University course in K. Chisholm and J. Ferguson, *Rome: the Augustan Age: a Source Book* (Oxford, 1981). Augustus' own account of himself is translated and excellently commented on by P.A. Brunt and J.M. Moore, *Res Gestae Divi Augusti: The Achievements of the Divine Augustus* (Oxford, 1970). Dio's Augustan narrative is available in Penguin, translated by I. Scott-Kilvert, with introduction by J.M. Carter; and translated in selection with commentary by J.W. Rich in the Aris and Phillips series (1990). For Plutarch on Antony, see C.B.R. Pelling, *Plutarch's Life of Antony* (Cambridge, 1988). Suetonius' life of Augustus is available in Robert Graves' Penguin translation, *The Twelve Caesars*; there is a good commentary by J.M. Carter in the Bristol Classical Press series (*Suetonius: Divus Augustus*, 1982). Ovid's *Art of Love* is well translated by Peter Green in Penguin (Ovid, *The Erotic Poems*, 1982). Virgil's *Aeneid* finds new translators in each generation: the latest are Robert Fitzgerald (in verse) and David West (in prose), both available in Penguin.

Also available in the Classical World Series

Greek Tragedy
An Introduction
Marion Baldock

In this introduction to Greek tragedy, which constitutes some of the most powerful drama of the Western world, the author traces its development and performance with detailed chapters on each of the three tragic poets – Aeschylus, Sophocles and Euripides. Specific plays and topics are considered, and one chapter compares the differing treatment of the 'Electra' theme by each dramatist.

With illustrations, quotations from the plays in English, an annotated bibliography and suggestions for further study, *Greek Tragedy* is an invaluable guide to a study of the tragic genre.

1-85399-119-8

Women in Classical Athens
Sue Blundell

While the men of Classical Athens were fighting wars and producing great works of art, what were the women doing? According to some male writers of the period, they were at home, making wool and babies; others thought they were more likely to be visiting their friends and partying until the small hours. This book investigates the many contrasting images of Athenian women which the Classical Age produced. Taking as its starting-point women in the Parthenon sculptures, it examines two levels of feminine experience: the human and the divine. The interplay between women's religious prominence and their domestic obscurity is discussed in relation to the young citizen women who lead the procession; while the great goddesses represented in the frieze are studied in terms of their relationships with human worshippers and, on a symbolic level, with the mythological females, such as the Amazons, who appear in the metopes. Finally, the book turns to a third aspect, looking at the women who do not appear in the Parthenon sculptures – the prostitutes, slaves and alien women who make a vital economic and ideological contribution to the Athenian achievement.

1-85399-543-6

The Roman Satirists and Their Masks
Susanna Morton Braund

This book presents an approach to Roman verse satire radically different from the usual chronological sequence that treats each poet in turn. Braund starts from the conviction that Latin literature gains from being viewed as performance and sees the creation of different 'masks' (*personae*) as a result of the Roman training in rhetoric. She treats the texts of Roman satire not as autobiography but as drama. Three main chapters examine the most prominent masks created by the satirical poets: the angry, the mocking, and the ironic characters. Illustrative material is drawn from the best-known satires, primarily of Horace and Juvenal. There follows analysis of the relationship between the satirist and society: does he belong in society or is he essentially an outsider? Braund then investigates the authority of the satirist, which makes satire seem at times so realistic, and finally she considers the relationship between satirists and their audiences; the genre of satire is tricky to interpret: is there, or can there ever be, a 'right' response to it?

Suggestions for further study and reading, a glossary of technical terms and an index of the poems discussed are provided. All texts are in English translation.

1-85399-139-2

Aristophanes and his Theatre of the Absurd
Paul Cartledge

Aristophanes, the Athenian comic dramatist, remains popular despite historical changes in attitude and belief. Placing the plays in their total civic, religious and dramatic context, this account explores their significance for contemporary audiences, and their continuing appeal. Separate chapters address aspects of his work and world, and outline the playwright's own opinions at a time of intense political debate.

With original texts quoted in translation this comprehensive and lively study will provide students with an invaluable insight into the plays and their place in classical Athens.

1-85399-114-7

Religion and the Romans
Ken Dowden

This book provides a short, action-packed modern introduction to religion in the Roman world. It deals with the public and private nature of religion at Rome itself, and looks at the native cults of the Empire, with special reference to Gaul, as well as considering how the exotic cults such as those of Isis and Mithras were viewed. Finally, a fresh look is taken at the conflict of Christianity with the inhabitants and authorities of the Empire – from Nero to Constantine and beyond.

This lively and accessible book will prove invaluable to students of the classical world providing a much-needed general survey of Roman religion.

1-85399-180-5

Morals and Values in Ancient Greece
John Ferguson

From the society of the Homeric poems through to the rise of Christianity, this account charts the progression of morals and values in the Greek world.

The author begins by discussing how a 'guilt-culture' superseded the old 'shame-culture' without totally displacing it. He then examines how democracy, the philosophers and finally Alexander's conquest influenced the values of the ancient Greeks.

Original texts are quoted in translation, and this clear, chronological study will provide an exciting introduction for students while offering experts a fresh approach to the subject.

1-85399-118-X

Slavery in Classical Greece
N.R.E. Fisher

This is an authoritative and clearly written account of the main issues involved in the study of Greek slavery from Homeric times to the fourth century BC. It provides valuable insights into the fundamental place of slavery in the economies and social life of classical Greece, and includes penetrating analyses of the widely-held ancient ideological justifications of slavery.

A wide range of topics is covered, including chapters on the development of slavery from Homer to the classical period, on the peculiar form of community slaves (the helots) found in Sparta, on the economic functions and the treatment of slaves in Athens, and on the evidence for slaves' resistance. Throughout, the book shows how political and economic systems, ideas of national identity, work and gender, and indeed the fundamental nature of Greek civilization itself, were all profoundly affected by the fact that many of the Greek city-states were slave societies.

1-85399-134-1

Art and the Romans
Anne Haward

There is more to Roman art than mosaics. What did the Romans look for in their portraits? Was there impressionist painting before the Impressionists? This survey for the general student looks at the art created for and by the Romans and what they wanted from it.

In place of the usual historical outline approach, *Art and the Romans* looks at the subject by genre; the Romans' appreciation of painting, sculpture and the decorative arts, in a society where the majority of work was commissioned, was different from that of the present day. Art for a world without printing or photography to spread visual images meant much more direct contact with the artist and influence by the patron. Drawing on literary sources as well as illustrations from many parts of the Roman world, this survey up to the time of Constantine considers what Romans hoped to achieve and how far they were successful. Included are suggestions for further study, a bibliography and recommended sites to view the art discussed.

1-85399-558-4

Roman Britain
S.J. Hill and S. Ireland

The Roman occupation of Britain lasted for nearly 400 years and produced a wide-ranging and radical transformation of the country, affecting virtually every aspect of life: town-development, transport, agriculture, industry and lifestyle. Rome also opened Britain to the intellectual and religious diversity of the empire. Yet there is plentiful evidence in both the literary record and the ever-increasing archaeological material to show that Britain – a late-comer to Rome's empire – often resisted external influence and imbued imported Roman ways with native characteristics.

The book introduces the history of Rome's involvement with Britain in a succinct but readable way, providing an overview of the country's already diverse culture before the advent of the legions; tracing the historical development of the province under Rome and how the Romans maintained their hold on it; and tackling topics such as administration, development of towns and the countryside, religion and art. The aim of the book is not simply to supply information, but to invite the reader to ask questions and delve deeper into Rome's most northerly province.

1-85399-140-6

Classical Epic: Homer and Virgil
Richard Jenkyns

In the ancient world Homer was recognised as the fountain-head of culture. His poems, the *Iliad* and the *Odyssey*, were universally admired as examples of great literature which could never be surpassed.

In this new study, Richard Jenkyns re-examines the two Homeric epics and the work that is perhaps their closest rival, the *Aeneid* of Virgil. A wide range of topics is covered, including chapters on heroism and tragedy in the *Iliad*, morality in the *Odyssey* and Virgil's skilful reworking of elements from the two earlier epics.

1-85399-133-3

The Environment and the Classical World
Patricia Jeskins

For the people of antiquity, the dominant force in shaping their life, economy and culture was the natural environment. This book explores the direct influence of the geography, climate and resources of the classical Mediterranean world upon the lives of the Greeks and Romans, and their ingenuity in exploiting that environment and meeting its challenges. Intended for A-level and undergraduate students, the book distils from the wide range of specialist sources a concise yet comprehensive introduction to Classical Studies; topics include settlements, politics, society, domestic life, religion, architecture, agriculture, crafts and trade, travel and warfare. Highly readable, well-illustrated, with useful maps, frequent reference to ancient sources, and guidance for further study, its systematic and lively approach will assist and stimulate those coming to the subject for the first time.

1-85399-547-9

Political Life in the City of Rome
John R. Patterson

Politicians of the Roman Republic employed techniques ranging from persuasive oratory through extravagant entertainment and bribery to lethal violence to get their way. Political rivalries were fought out on the streets of Rome and in the popular assemblies as much as in the Senate House. This new book looks at the Roman political system (how did it work? how much influence did ordinary Romans have?) and examines the practicalities of politics – how politicians persuaded the voters to support their candidates or proposals – in Rome in the period 200-50 BC. A central theme is the topography of the city of Rome and the ways in which political rivalries transformed the appearance of the city.

There is a wealth of recent and important scholarly research in these areas and this study aims to make the material and the debates to which it relates – especially discussions of Roman topography – more accessible to both sixth-formers and undergraduates.

1-85399-514-2

Greece and the Persians
John Sharwood Smith

This account traces each stage of the critical struggle between the Persian Empire and the early Greek states, from the first clashes to the miraculous return home of 10,000 Greek mercenaries stranded in the heart of Persia. Carefully examining sources and placing events within their geographical and historical contexts, the author attempts to define cultural and political differences between the two peoples. His balanced questioning approach places fresh emphasis on the Persian perspective and provides an accessible and informed introduction to the period.

1-85399-113-9

Athens Under the Tyrants
J.A. Smith

This study focuses on the colourful period of the Peisistratid tyranny in Athens. During these exciting years the great festivals were established, monumental buildings were erected, the population grew rapidly and there was lively progress in all the arts.

This study considers the artistic, archaeological and literary evidence for the period. Athens is seen largely through the eyes of Herodotus, the 'Father of History', and we can observe the foundations being laid for the growth of democracy in the following century.

1-85399-116-3

Athens and Sparta
S.C. Todd

Conservative Sparta and democratic Athens were the main rivals for the leadership of the Classical Greek world. Unlike many introductions to the subject which concentrate on historical narrative, *Athens and Sparta* focuses particularly on the image of the two societies. This gives the book an unusual breadth in chronology and subject matter. Topics include education, land-holding, politics, and the division between the sexes. There are chapters on Thucydides and the Peloponnesian War, and on Greece under Roman rule.

This stimulating book contains more than twenty photographs, maps and drawings, and assumes no previous knowledge of Greek history.

1-85399-398-0

Greek Architecture
R.A. Tomlinson

Greek Architecture is a clearly structured discussion of all the major buildings constructed by the Greeks, from houses to temples, theatres to Council buildings.

This book describes particular architectural styles and features and sets the buildings in their context, with an evaluation of their purpose, siting and planning. With over 40 illustrations enhancing the text, *Greek Architecture* provides an informed and comprehensive view of the design and function of buildings in ancient Greece.

1-85399-115-5

Cities of Legend
The Mycenaean World
K.A. & Diana Wardle

Little over one hundred years has passed since Schliemann first excavated at Mycenae and revealed the riches of its rulers, buried in the Shaft Graves three and a half thousand years ago. Continuing discoveries have demonstrated the achievements and connections of Mycenaean civilization. The decipherment of their script, Linear B, as an early form of Greek, has shown that the Mycenaeans were the ancestors of the Greeks of the Classical period and has revealed the complex administration of their palaces.

This introduction to the Mycenaean world brings together the latest research to provide a clear account of its history and of the real Bronze Age cities which lie behind the Homeric legends. Mycenaean economy and society, technology and trade, burials and buildings, warfare and religion are all explored in illustrating the character and achievements of this brilliant forerunner of Classical Greece. The final chapter is devoted to the no-longer-so Dark Age, during which Greek society was transformed and the Homeric epic reached its final form.

1-85399-355-7

The Julio-Claudian Emperors
Thomas Wiedemann

'The dark, unrelenting Tiberius, the furious Caligula, the feeble Claudius, the profligate and cruel Nero...are condemned to everlasting infamy' wrote Gibbon. This 'infamy' has inspired the work of historians and novelists from Roman times to the present.

This book summarises political events during the reigns of Tiberius, Caligula, Claudius and Nero, and the civil wars of the 'year of four emperors'. It considers too the extent to which social factors influenced the imperial household.

Assuming no knowledge of Latin and drawing on material including inscriptions and coins, literary history and the latest historical interpretations, the author presents a coherent account of the often apparently erratic actions of these emperors.

1-85399-117-1

For further details of these and other Bristol Classical Press books please contact:

Gerald Duckworth & Co. Ltd
61 Frith Street
London W1D 3JL
Tel: 020 7434 4242
Fax: 020 7434 4420
e-mail: inquiries@duckworth-publishers.co.uk
Website: www.ducknet.co.uk